The Eggshell Path
A Story of Survival

The Eggshell Path

A Story of Survival

VALERIE PAGET-WILKES

SEVEN LOCKS PRESS

Santa Ana, California

Seven Locks Press
P.O. Box 25689
Santa Ana, CA 92799
(800) 354-5348

Individual sales: This book is available through most bookstores or can be ordered directly from Seven Locks Press at the address above.

Quantity Sales: Special discounts are available on quantity purchases by corporations, associations and others. For details, contact the "Special Sales Department" at the publisher's address above.

Printed in the United States of America

Library of Congress Cataloging-in-Publication Data is available from the publisher

ISBN: 978-0-9790950-9-2

www.eggshellpath.com

For my beloved daughters
Helen and Gail and Megan
and
to mothers everywhere
who have lost a child

Closure

If I close my eyes do I lose sight of her? No, quite the opposite — she becomes vivid in my imagination, her very existence a breath away.

Why the need for closure? What is this word?

Cessation. Discontinuance. To shut out or bring to an end. A dead stop; yes it was definitely that.

What am I to put to rest?

Her molecular being has long gone, her soul I'm sure is on the second circuit of the everlasting track.

What am I to close? That she once was? Am I ending my grief?

Sorrow has a beginning, but its end is limitless. How can you cap off the emotional well of a lifetime of memories? The broken heart still bleeds. The agony of departure still real.

Suffering diminishes slowly, at times imperceptibly. Sometimes it is so encompassing and lasting, it feels like terror. It can never be erased as abruptly as the word closure might suggest.

It's over. We've neatly packed up all prostrations of grief into a coffin labeled "closed".

Cease, desist — no more. Enough!

Closure, a nonsensical word of modern times for the convenience of others.

A pox on others.

Conclusion? I know what it is. It's in the instant of knowing.

Chapter One

The alarm went off as usual at five-fifteen that morning, forcing me to wake. Convinced I'd only been asleep for five minutes, I recalled the nagging, unfathomable thoughts of trying to get to sleep during the night. Thoughts that later refused to form into a proper dream. Always on the edge of sleep, I seemed to be looking in on myself.

An eerie, silent uneasiness crept over me as I got out of bed to go to the bathroom. The house was too quiet, and seemed to harken back to the dream. The non-existent dream. I crossed to the other end of the house and ran down the corridor, to check what I instinctively knew would be ominously empty bedrooms.

Where were they?

Megan and her four friends visiting from Ohio had left yesterday afternoon for the beach, but should have been home hours ago. Despite the early hour, I called Giles.

"Hmm yes? Hello," was the sleepy response. I didn't care that I'd woken him up; he was Megan's father after all, and if I was worried then he should be too. This strange queasy notion was getting a grip. I quickly told him the girls weren't home and asked if they were with him.

"No," he said. "But don't worry, they probably stayed over."

"But this isn't like Megan," I replied. "She always calls to let me know where she is."

"Well," he said. "There's not much we can do at this hour. Go to school. Call me later if you get an opportunity, or I'll try to get in touch with you if I hear anything."

Un-reassured, I hung up the phone. With a heavy heart, I started the routine ablutions before I made the twenty-mile journey to the hospital, where I would start a new rotation in heart surgery. Although I was an English-trained nurse, I was three-quarters of the way through a year's extra schooling to become a surgical technician enabling me to work in the operating room.

"Good morning, Mum," I said aloud in my darkened car, as I weaved in and out of the moderate traffic, thankfully not having to compete with other early morning commuters also bent on beating the customary snarl-up yet to come on that main artery to town.

Artery! Hey! That's good.

If I'm going south, it must be the aorta I'm traveling on; north would be the inferior vena cava and I likened all the off roads to the main arterial branches as I tried to visualize the anatomy of the heart and the surrounding vessels in preparation for my day.

And then there was my mother.

Should I say "Happy anniversary?" "Happy death day?" "How the hell are you?" "Sorry for me day" "What's it like out there?"

I pondered this dilemma as I drove, and came to the conclusion that my dear old Mum would be touched and delighted enough that I had even remembered this tenth anniversary of her death. Mother, I miss you so, and you're still part of my heart.

The heart is both an electrical and mechanical pump, and I have often wondered why it has been equated with "love". I suppose it's more appealing than, say an elbow or a liver, and God knew not to choose either sex organ. I shuddered at those images flashing before me, for in plain truth, both are bloody ugly.

Liver, lover, it might have worked.

I turned off the main blood vessel route to one of the coronary arteries and greeted Kathy, my partner and friend at our usual spot in the parking lot.

"Hi," she said. "You're late this morning! Are you ready to be a heart scrub today?"

"I would be, if that little brat of mine had come home last night."

She chuckled in reply and empathy, because during the last three days I'd been telling her how five eighteen-year-old girls had transformed my perfectly normal neat and tidy house into a chaotic mass of overflowing suitcases, rumpled clothes, wet towels, empty styrofoam cups and bubble gum wrappers. The bathrooms were a disastrous mess of hairdryer and curling iron cords, unstoppered toothpaste tubes, make-up kits and open drawers. Why didn't these girls ever close anything?

There was hardly a square inch of floor space to be seen, and I openly praised the inventor of the split plan for homes, as my bedroom was strictly off limits. If the demons didn't invade my space, I could just about tolerate five teenagers for the week of Spring Break.

Megan had spent her junior year in high school in a small town in Ohio. She was sixteen, and well into the "I know everything- what do you know- you can't tell me what to do- I hate you more than ever, Mother" mode. Her moods were so mercurial; it was I who hurtled on the emotional roller coaster. In fact I was on my own pre-hysterectomy agenda. Coupled with the stress of a dissolving marriage, I often got confused about who I was supposed to be, mother or daughter.

She was typical of course, one minute in floods of tears because she couldn't understand "stupid" Shakespeare, and the next giggling hysterically because she couldn't read her own handwriting.

Penmanship was never at the top of her list of priorities, and I was often asked to decipher a word that resembled a daddy longlegs, which sent us both off into peals of laughter.

"Why do I have to learn this stuff?" she would say of anything that didn't interest her, "I'm never going to need it." Indeed, her grades went from A to F just I think, to stop me from getting bored, and the weekly trips to the school guidance counselor had become routine. I had long given up making any comment on her appearance, preferring to keep my opinions to myself on the ghoulish eye make-up, or the belly dancer midriffs.

So, it was either a murder/suicide pact to put us both out of misery, or send her away with as much space between us as possible. I decided I really did love her very much, and thought she would eventually be worth keeping, so distance was the immediate answer.

Her eldest sister, Helen, was in her final year at college in a very tiny town in the middle of nowhere in Ohio. She suggested that Megan could live with her; she felt sure she'd be better able to cope than me, and having gone to college herself on a swimming scholarship, understood the needs of the champion swimmer Megan was destined to be.

"It will be a good sister bonding time," Helen had said. "And Eric can help with swimming and her homework. You need a break. We'll take care of her."

Eric, also a swimmer, was Helen's boyfriend, and as he was the youngest of eight children, a lad with five sisters, I thought him more than able to accommodate and tolerate another one.

Megan had been excited about the prospect of leaving home, so she, Giles and I made the long journey from Florida to Ohio on a fact-finding trip to interview the local high school principal, but more importantly the swimming coach. Bob would later prove to be the best coach Megan had ever had, and she raced to Olympic times she never thought possible.

She thoroughly enjoyed her year up north, made lots of friends and lasting impressions on everyone, but was glad to come home for her senior year. Now a year later, four of her closest girlfriends had driven south to spend their Spring Break with us. An eighteen-hour drive that was loyalty beyond the 'free beer' giveaway that resulted in Megan being fired from her waitressing job at Pizza Hut.

"For all her faults," I told Kathy as we walked into the O.R. locker rooms to change. "Megan will always call me to at least let me know where she is."

We searched through the piles of clean scrubs to find our respective sizes.

"If she's late," I went on. "She seems to think that calling will somehow exonerate the crime and I'll forget, which more often than not is true. It's so hard keeping up with kids when they have their own car."

"I'm dreading it," Kathy moaned. "Rachel's almost fifteen, and is already begging me to let her drive on back roads."

"Well," said I. "It's not all bad. I know Megan's a good driver when she concentrates long enough, and at least now I'm spared the drudge of driving her to swim practice every day."

We made our way to the front desk to get our assignments for the day. Shortly thereafter, I grabbed a moment to call Giles. He'd gone to work early and answered on the first ring. No, he said, he hadn't heard a word from Megan.

By the time I'd reached my designated operating room, the surgical nurses had things well under way. Judging by the amount of equipment and instruments already in place, some pretty neat plumbing jobs could have taken place. For my part I clung to the walls in fear of being asked to do anything. It was here I stayed until after the patient was brought into the room and the operation started.

Before any work on the heart can begin, patients have to be connected to a perfusion machine; a series of tubes and pumps enabling blood to reach the rest of the body while the heart is stopped. I stared in awe as blood left the fuselage and traveled halfway around the room on its circuit through these pipes. Amazing!

The patient would never know he'd just gone on a little walkabout without taking a step.

Curiosity and fascination were getting the better of me, so I inched forward in an effort to see. And what a sight it was! It was like a scene out of a horror movie, a poor guy's chest opened to the elements with a chain saw, and now, four people were periodically dipping their bloody hands into the cavity to retrieve another treasure. The atmosphere however, was serene with Debussy softly playing, and I marveled at the competency of the doctors.

After a while, the head surgeon beckoned me over.

"I need you to be chief heart holder today," he said. "Come up here beside me."

Oh my! I glanced up at the clock as I squeezed between two green-clad figures to the head of the table.

A quarter to ten.

I didn't know quite what to expect as I peered into the gaping hole and saw this essential blob for the first time. This heart looked so forlorn in its silent, still state, that I felt it should have had "LOVE" etched on its pericardium; something to make it seem real.

With some trepidation I placed my hand over the surgeon's as he gently guided my fingers to serve as a retractor over the life's force of someone I didn't know. Such an enormous responsibility for someone so new, that I was humbled by the experience. I'd never met anyone in that room until today. No introductions are necessary between behind the scenes technicians and patients in an operating room. And yet here I was holding the indispensable organ of life and marveling at the blind trust placed upon me. One false move and the fragile light would be snuffed out forever. I was struck by the sense of mortality and how flimsy the link between life and death really is.

A little while later I was sent out for a coffee break. The intense concentration had left me with a headache, so I sought out fresh air and relaxing company. I caught up with Kathy.

"Hey! This is absolutely awesome," I told her as we exchanged viewpoints. "But do you know," I went on. "The strangest thing happened." I related how I'd looked up to the clock mid-morning. "This was the moment my mother died, isn't that odd? But then again I don't know why I should be so surprised, because she and I always shared incredible telepathy, which I suppose continues beyond the grave."

Kathy's mother had passed away three months earlier of lung cancer, the same illness that had claimed mine. The two of us sat there in blessed harmony, in mutual respect, mourning the losses of beloved mothers, one very recent, one long gone. But we had to get back to our respective operating rooms.

Chapter Two

Our day finished at one o'clock.

"I'm exhausted," I said to Kathy on the reverse trip to the parking lot. "Both physically and mentally. I'll have to take a nap this afternoon. See you tomorrow."

It was a glorious spring day as I made my way back on the long arterial road, declogged of clots at that time. Once more I conversed with my mother's spirit.

"You would have been proud of me today Mum," I said out loud. "It was so thrilling, I can hardly stand the excitement. Only three more months of school. Yippee!"

I began to think about my future and the upcoming weekend. House hunting.

Although Giles had always been a good provider, I was unable to accommodate the cold, selfish person he'd become. We'd been separated for a year. He'd rented a second story apartment in a complex just five minutes away. Hardly apart, it was ridiculous. We talked on the phone every day, walked the dogs every weekend, and he was always at the house for a meal or two in between. A fluid understanding settled over us. It was at my urging that we decided to give our marriage another try. The big house was up for sale and we were looking to buy a smaller property in the country.

As I thought about the house, I wondered if the girls were home yet. The same odd sensation I'd had on waking this morning returned. What was this uneasy feeling? I put it down to the fact it was the anniversary of my mother's death, and that I was pretty much emotionally spent having witnessed such awesome affairs of the heart all morning long.

My thoughts drifted back to the previous afternoon when Megan, clad only in a bikini, had all four doors of her Toyota Corolla opened and piles of beach gear strewn over the grass and driveway like a midweek yard sale in progress.

"Please, Megan," I had said. "Some people are coming to see the house later this afternoon. I must ask you to clear this mess up. It doesn't give a very good first impression. It's the curbside appeal that sells a house you know. And please turn the radio down a bit."

"Chill, Mom."

I winced at this expression, but made no comment.

"We'll be out of here very soon, and if people come to see the house, they'll just have to go around us. It's no big deal."

Maybe not to you I thought, but again kept silent. It was no use arguing, she obviously wasn't going to hurry, and talking back only triggered a deliberate slow. I tried another tack.

"Let me help you with these towels, —Megan, please don't take that good one to the beach."

"Mom, please don't be so fussy. A little sand won't hurt it." I stood helplessly by as one of my best scotch plaid towels disappeared into the boot of the car.

The other girls joined Megan, and the car gradually filled with duffel bags, coolers, and goodness knows what else.

Good grief, how long are these girls going to be gone?

To my relief, they eventually were ready to leave, and fortunately before potential house buyers began arriving.

"Look, Mom," said Megan grinning up to me from the driver's seat. "Aren't you proud of me wearing my seatbelt? And I make the others wear theirs too, even in the backseat."

"That's great! Well drive carefully, enjoy yourselves, but don't be too late."

"Mom!" Again that petulant tone.

OK. OK. and they were gone in a cloud of dust with blaring music and squeals of laughter.

Almost home. I turned the last corner to my road and frowned slightly as I could see that the car from Ohio and not Megan's was the only one in the driveway. Not home yet?

I greeted Thatcher, my lovely springer spaniel, and his three-legged black retriever friend Liza.

"Hi guys! Where's that naughty Megan?"

I entered the kitchen and was relieved to see the flashing light of the answering machine. It was Giles' short message. "Call me as soon as you get home, please."

I put the kettle on to make tea and then dialed his office number. Giles was at home, I was told. I idly thought, Strange, he's home at this time of day, and then became irritated when I believed "this" was his home and he wasn't here.

I made another call to Giles "at home" and he answered immediately.

"Uh—we have a potentially serious problem with Megan—she's been involved in a car accident."

"What? How bad of an accident? Is she all right? Where is she?"

"I don't know any details, but apparently someone called Gail around eleven o'clock this morning. Why? I don't know. . . Uh-oh, I see a police car. . ."

"I'll be right there." And I vaguely heard him say, "drive carefully" as I slammed down the phone and rushed out of the house.

Oh no, oh no, please, dear God. Please!

My heart was pounding. My head spun as I roared around the first corner, my back tires making wheelies in the dirt.

"Get out of my way," I said to no one. I lived in an isolated area and fortunately there wasn't another car in sight. I gripped the steering wheel tighter and drove like a maniac until I was forced to stop at a traffic light.

Come on, come on. Move! Red to green and I careened on motoring at a horrendous pace in a twenty-five mile an hour zone. Just let the police stop me now as I flew past their favorite place for catching speeders. It was vacant.

I felt sick. The acid contents of my empty stomach rose to the back of my throat. *Swallow, breathe.*

Another traffic light slowed me to a halt.

Oh no, no, please don't let my worst fears be true.

Just let her be seriously hurt, maybe in a coma for a while; we can fix that. She's such a fine athlete, so physically strong; she can overcome any injury. Please, dear God.

I had turned into the apartment complex and saw the oncoming police car. There was no point in flagging him down; I was almost at Giles' "home". I glanced at the driver in passing, young, fresh-faced, clean-shaven. Inexperienced? Maybe he's got it all wrong.

Look out!

Why was I in such a rush to hear what I instinctively knew to be true? I wanted to scream; I wanted to rock back and forth; I wanted to run, hide, escape. I wanted my Mummy.

Oh God, help me!

Forced to slow down for the speed bumps (remember how you laughed, Megan, when Daddy called them "sleeping policemen") and I was there. Cutting off the paths that divided the apartments, in one last pathetic attempt to shorten the journey, I ran across the grass and up the stairs two at a time.

I glanced up to see Giles silhouetted in the doorway.

Chapter Three

He stepped back into his apartment as I flew through the door. "She's dead."

"NOOOOOOO," I screamed as Giles gathered me up in his arms. "NOOOOO"

No,no,no, over and over again, and once more, NO!

And then I was standing in a black cylinder of construction paper, with my arms straight over my head. It was very dark, but I looked up to see a solitary round cut diamond twinkling a kaleidoscope of brilliant white lights. As it dipped towards me, it blinded me with a changing hue of pinks, blues and purple with each faceted turn, until it settled on my left cheek.

A nano second later, with startling actuality I realized a button from Giles' shirt was pressing into my face as he held me ever so tightly.

I sobbed, free falling tears as I desperately struggled to assimilate the devastating news. A split second of calm.

How dare he tell me she's dead just like that. Couldn't he have at least softened the blow.

Told me to sit down or something.

Gasping for air, I broke free from his embrace, but continued to stand close.

With tears streaming down my face, I looked at him and said," I'm so very sorry." Giles said nothing, but stared back at me with unreadable eyes.

I was compelled to move as the next wave of realization hit me like a giant slap to the side of my head. This can't be true.

Pacing, pacing. Oh no! My darling Megan. My baby. Please wait, I haven't finished telling you all I know.

I sat, I stood, and I flailed, all the while shaking my head in constant denial.

Please don't let this be true. It just cannot be.

Meggie!

Mighty Megan Mega Mouth, the fitting nickname bestowed upon her since the sixth grade was silenced. Oh, such pain—it hurt me so. This was more than I could bear.

Giles let me ramble for a few more seconds before he told me a second girl had also died in the accident. What! Oh dear God this was too much.

"Who?" I asked, desperately trying to visualize their faces.

"I can't remember the name," said Giles. "Jennifer is it, or maybe Heather."

Oh Lord! Which one was Heather? All I could see was a mass of vibrant humanity dancing in the living room less than twenty-four hours ago, now blurred into one.

"What the hell happened?"

I was slightly calmer now and wanted details.

"All the police have told me so far is that Megan's car ran off the road on Interstate 95 just south of Daytona about nine o'clock this morning; no other vehicle was involved, but two people died and three have been taken to the hospital. They apparently called Gail asking her if she was Megan's sister. When Gail said yes, all the caller would say was "we'll call you back". Gail's been frantically calling me wanting to know what's going on. Of course," Giles continued. "I didn't know anything until just now. We'd better call her—and Helen."

Breathe, I told myself; take slow deep breaths. Remember your training for treating shock. But the prospect of telling my daughters their sister was dead made me hyperventilate more.

"Do you want me to call?" Giles asked.

I shouted back at him, "I will."

Maybe I was a little too vehement but it was a mother thing; the umbilical cord severed forever. I lost sight of the fact that he was also their parent. At that time, it didn't occur to me that he was in shock too. Where were his tears? I selfishly couldn't help feeling as fiercely protective as a wild cat losing one of her offspring.

I closed my eyes. Think what you're going to say. It has to be gentle, but there is no easy way. Dead? Died? Deceased? Passed on? Never! I hate that expression. Killed? Sweet Jesus! How on earth am I going to do this? Tears started afresh as the awful truth began to dawn on me.

Giles came up beside me and put his arm around my shoulder.

"I'll get in touch with Carl," he said. "I know he'll be able to help."

Carl, a patrol officer, an offbeat biker, a whacky, gruff, daredevil sort of guy with a well-concealed huge heart who absolutely adored Megan. Yes, he's a good person to know at a time like this.

I waited for a spasm of nausea to subside.

Control yourself; focus; you have to do this. The girls trust you; you must stay strong for them.

I yearned to have both of them in my arms, I needed their support.

Death is a debilitating equalizer. Who is the mother and who is the child now? Surely, we were all mixed up in a tangle of cords, never to be the same again.

I'd suffered an attack of my heart, leaving me emotionally toxic. Would I have enough adrenalin running through my veins to cope?

I made my way to the kitchen and the telephone.

Giles came up beside me and asked, "Do you know how you're going to tell them?"

"No," I said. "But I will."

Are you kidding? How can anyone be prepared for this? Maybe the Queen. I'm told she travels everywhere with a black ensemble and a speech just in case.

I stared down at the two overripe bananas on the counter top. My eyes were riveted on the longitudinal brown lines turning to black and the different shades of tan spots making a pattern resembling a leopard's skin. The practical side of my brain told me if they weren't eaten soon, they would rot and die; disintegrate; return to nothing. I felt like smashing them then and there. Go to God with Megan.

I picked up the telephone. Number one, Helen in Chicago. First born, stable, fiercely ambitious and unselfishly compassionate. She'd hardly been a child. At all important stages of her life she seemed to have read the book before I did. I never had to worry about her, and needed her to be my rock now. She was almost finished studying for her Master's degree in Forensic Science. I hoped this would be the easier call, a practice run for Gail. Helen was rarely home because of job and university commitments. I was lucky she answered the phone. Lucky? There was no luck involved today.

"Hi Mom, how are you?" cheerful as usual. *Oh God give me strength.*

"Helen."

She knew instantly something was wrong.

"Mom! What's the matter?"

The words came spilling out, "Megan's been involved in a car accident—Helen—I want you to sit down—Oh God—I'm so sorry darling—she's been killed."

Helen's "NO" echoed mine and together we cried and we cried. We were indivisible through tears, the geographic distance abridged by sorrow. Minutes later we babbled. Each one of us vainly tried to comfort the other in a confusion of words and sobs. I told her every sketchy detail, including the second death. Helen was acquainted with all Megan's Ohio friends, but there were so many, she had difficulty remembering if she'd ever met Heather. I knew she would want to talk to her father, so handed the phone to Giles, who in his own pragmatic way told her he would ask his secretary Rosa to make airline reservations as soon as possible.

I urged Helen to contact a good friend, anyone she could feel comfortable with at a time like this.

"Please don't be alone, and promise me you'll call every hour if it gets too much for you. Will you call Eric, or would you like me to do that?"

"No, I'll tell him," she said. Complete desolation in her voice; such a huge responsibility to undertake for someone so young.

Both of us were reluctant to say goodbye, but what more could be said?

"Let's hope you can get a flight tonight. Until then my darling, I love you so. Bye."

I wept.

Poor Giles, he had no idea what to do with me. The intimacy that should have been there between us, as parents, at a time like this was awkwardly missing. We were being forced into a situation that was too much of a shock to understand immediately. The necessary speed needed to cope with this was beyond our fragile marital skills. Giles did his best to console the inconsolable. Knowing men are much more task than relationship orientated, I could see he would be more comfortable if he had something to do.

"Dial Gail's number," I told him. "But please let me talk to her first."

Gail's relationship with her father was tenuous at best. We, on the other hand, were more like twin sisters. I knew she would want to hear this from me.

At twenty-one, having spent the last four years struggling to find her identity at college, with no clue to her future career, we had spent hours soul searching, putting family and the world to rights.

Gail was three years older than Megan, and had a tremendous influence on her. Gone were the bratty, spiteful fights between young sisters, often physical, but more often verbal with horrible sarcastic remarks from Gail, countered with witty and funny comments from Megan. They had grown to truly love each other.

"Mom! What the hell is going on?" Gail's shrill voice broke up the musings. "What's up with Megan? The police called me this morning. . ."

I interrupted her. "Gail—Oh God, Gail." She in turn cut me off, screaming now.

"Mom! Tell me. It is Megan isn't it? What's happening?"

The rising pitch of her voice and the increased panic somehow made me calmer. Adrenaline kicked in with a rush for a fight or flight situation as I struggled to stay composed.

"Yes," I said. "And there's no easy way of telling you this but…" I took in a deep breath and let out an audible sigh. "Gail, my darling girl, how I wish I could be there in person with you—*Help me, God please.* Megan was killed in a car crash this morning."

The unexpected silence on the other end of the phone unnerved me more than the screaming. Give me hysteria. Having raised three girls I could always cope with that.

"Gail," I whispered. "I'm so sorry. Gail? Gail are you there?"

All I could hear was a buzz of silence and then an enormous groan, hardly human.

I could sense she'd slumped, and now it was my turn to panic. Was she alone? Had she passed out? A blanket of guilt covered me. How could I do this to her? I should have been there to catch her fallen response. I knew how emotionally delicate she was.

"Gail?" I ventured.

"I'm here, Mom."

I heard her crying now, thank God for tears.

"Are you sure this is true?" she asked. "What happened?"

Again, as I had explained to her sister a few minutes beforehand, I told her all the details I knew.

"Does Helen know?"

"Yes," I said. "Hopefully she'll be able to get on a flight tonight. Dad's organizing that. Listen to me Gail; you must not be alone right now. Call one of your friends and get them to drive you down. We're leaving Dad's apartment and going over to the big house shortly, there's nothing more to be done here." I was crying again now, shameless tears puddling around my nose and dripping off the end of my chin. I staunched the flow with a swipe from the back of my hand. Gail and I sniffed in unison.

"Do you want to talk to your father?"

"No, not right now." I was glad Giles didn't hear this when he came from the bathroom offering me a tissue. No, not a tissue, he would never have such a feminine thing in his apartment, it was a wad of toilet paper, but I took it all the same.

"Gail," I said after a while. "Promise me you won't drink and drive. Please call Keri or Nicole, anyone who is willing to bring you down. I need you here with me as soon as you can make it. I love you so much, please take care."

"O.K. Mom," barely audible. "I'll see you shortly. Bye."

I sent up a silent prayer to keep her safe, and to see the wisdom of temporarily giving up that hard fought for independence to let someone else drive. Jacksonville was only two hours away, but for Gail to drive so shocked was another disaster in the offing.

Giles and I looked at each other; our faces mirroring the same disbelief, the same confused despondency. Overwhelming sorrow plunged us into an ethereal cocoon of despair. What were we to do? How would we cope with this?

"We'd better go home," I said.

"I'll call Carl from my cell phone and meet you over there," Giles replied as he led me out of his apartment and down the stairs.

The journey back to the house was far different this time. I should have received a ticket for driving too slowly. Everything seemed to be in slow motion; my arms weighed a stone and my legs were reluctant to move. I wanted to close my heavy eyelids and sleep, just drift off and perhaps with luck never wake again.

Every few seconds in my peripheral vision, I could see Megan, running beside the car, striding along with the grace of a gazelle, her long ponytail almost horizontal behind her as she effortlessly kept up with me. She used to run between the two homes as part of her training schedule.

"Used to". Oh my God, would I ever get "used to" saying that?

I realized I'd come to the traffic light and automatically turned left. Megan must have gone straight on because all I could see now were the trees lining the dirt road.

Strange thoughts jostled for priority in my addled brain.

My principal heart holder was gone and what's more she had taken the vital half of my force with her. I will then slowly bleed till my own death. I knew it.

Chapter Four

Drat! The pothole I usually managed to avoid jumped out at me and I felt the jolt on the undercarriage of the car. I turned into my driveway and noticed that in my haste to leave, I'd left the garage door open. Oh well, who cares?

My dogs greeted me as if I'd been gone a week not just an hour. The normalcy of this was wonderfully comforting and I knelt to give each one of them a hug. I ordered my mind to register those fatal words, and out loud tested my voice on my canine friends. "Megan's dead." No, no it didn't ring true; just because I said it you don't have to believe me. It's all a terrible mistake, a look-alike error. I looked up to the heavens, choking back tears. Megan.

The phone rang and with the same slow motion speed I begrudgingly went inside. It was Kathy.

"I knew you were more worried about Megan than you let on this morning, so I thought I'd call to see if everything's O.K.?"

"Oh Kathy—you must have known—Megan was killed in a car crash this morning."

There was the longest pause before Kathy spoke, I could hear her tears as she asked "How? Where? No I mean—Oh my God, I'm so sorry. What—is there anything I can do?"

"I don't know, I can't think straight right now, maybe later but thanks. I'll call you when I know a bit more."

Giles had arrived and was making tea as the phone rang again.

"I'm going to change out of my scrubs, you answer it." I wanted to hide in my closet and never come out. Cancel the rest of the day; indeed cancel the rest of my life.

Giles was still talking on the telephone when I finally returned to the kitchen.

Now the other phone was ringing. Megan's line. I ignored it; I couldn't face any of her friends yet. Let me find out what happened first; I needed details. And where were the other three girls?

I stared down at the cup of tea Giles had poured for me, but didn't touch it. Bugger the English with their propensity for the cure-all tea.

I was half listening to his conversation with whomever, until I heard him say "Are you sure Megan wasn't driving?" *Oh dear Lord, please forgive me, but perhaps You could let someone else be dead. Maybe it wasn't even Megan's car. It's all a mistake.*

I realized I was holding my breath. Giles was looking at me now and shaking his head. He hung up the phone.

"That was Carl," he said. "According to the initial police report, Heather was the other girl who died, and she was driving. Megan was the front seat passenger. The three girls were taken to Halifax Hospital in Daytona—pretty smashed up but alive, although one of them is critical. Apparently, there was an eye-witness who said the car just skidded off the road into the center median. Fortunately I suppose, no other vehicle was involved, and nobody's sure at this stage if a tire blew out or what happened. What I don't understand is where they were—several miles south of the turning to Orlando."

"Are they positive it was Megan's car?" Still that faint possibility. "Yes, a green Toyota Corolla." Hopes dashed yet again.

Giles continued, "Carl's going to go over there when he's finished his shift and talk to a buddy of his who's stationed in Daytona. I think James is in that area today; I'll call him, he might have some clout at the hospital to get us some information."

James was a pharmaceutical rep., and a very good friend to Giles and us all. Both belonged to a running group; a generous term for a mildly athletic bunch of people from all walks of life, who regularly met for a hare and hounds type run, followed by a marathon stint in the pub. In fact, it would be better to say it was a drinking club with a running problem! I didn't go every week, but sometimes the run would be a family one when the girls came with us. Megan especially took delight in overtaking rotund puffing forty-year olds, where she would blatantly deride the slow pokes bringing up the rear of the pack, especially James. However, to a man, everyone appreciated her athleticism and avidly followed her swimming progress.

"Drink your tea," said Giles. "Before it gets too cold. I'll try to get in touch with James."

"Please do that on your cell phone," I replied. "I need to call Ann."

I couldn't yet bear to go down the corridor to Megan's room to use her phone, and Giles, hearing the tone in my voice, wisely did not argue.

Ann worked for a college professor during the week, and on weekends tended bar at a local steak house. I worked there too, part-time, to help pay my way through school. Megan was also employed there, but not very often because of high school commitments. Whenever Megan and I worked together I kept one eye on her, and bailed her out of many a mishap.

"Mom!" she would say. "Quick, help me out. I'm in the weeds, please take water to table seventeen." Or "What should I do? I forgot to put the order in."

"Megs," the cook would bellow. "You've done it again, and I'm not happy."

Meanwhile Megan would sheepishly slink out of the kitchen behind me.

But it was Ann who took her under her wing, patiently guiding her through the joys of cocktailing. What laughs we had with Megan's tongue-tied versions of the alcoholic concoctions.

Another arse-gropper please.

Ann, my dearest friend, if ever I needed you, it's surely now.

". . .I'll be right there." Was all I heard her say, as I hung up the phone.

I stared out of the huge picture window in the living room. When would I comprehend the enormity of this situation? Tears coursed down my face as I watched a pair of mocking birds frolicking among the branches of the old cypress tree. I glanced down, and sure enough there was Roger, my cherished cat lurking at the base of the tree not missing a beat.

Meg, do you remember when we found Roger? An estimated three-week old kitten, obviously abandoned and screaming for his mother. Do you remember how we told you mother cats lick the bottoms of their babies to make them poo, and in order for him to survive, you would have to do the same!

The jangling ring of the phone startled me and I automatically answered it. This time my nursing teacher Betty.

"My dear," she said. "I've just heard the dreadful news from Kathy, I'm so very sorry. Is there anything I can do?"

"No," I sniffed, but before I could go on, she asked me. "Would you like me to get in touch with Trevor, the Translife guy who came to talk to us last week?"

Was it really only a week ago I'd been so fascinated with the lecture on organ donation and tissue harvesting, that I thought it might have been something I'd like to pursue. But on my own daughter? Oh God, oh dear Lord—a fresh flood of tears. Now it was all real.

The spark of truth reassembled some practical order in my brain.

"Yes" I said to Betty, and the stronger the notion dawned that Megan's magnificent body could contribute to another living soul, the more passionate I became on making this happen.

"Yes," I said again, more vehemently this time.

"Where is she?"

"I don't know! I don't know anything, but that it was a single vehicle accident, and one of Megan's friends also died. The three survivors have been taken to Halifax Hospital in Daytona."

"I'll take care of it," Betty told me. "Leave everything to me, I know Trevor very well and I know he'll do his best."

Take charge Betty. But I was glad, because now there was just a glimmer of positive mitigation. I knew there couldn't be any way to retrieve post-mortem internal organs, but there was so much more—bone, skin, corneas and those precious heart valves. Megan, so young and fit and healthy had so much to offer even in death.

I took a deep breath. Good, something was being done. What next?

The phone rang again. It was Gail.

"Mom, how you doing?" A voice thick with crying, but no matter, she was alive.

"I just want to tell you, Scott will be calling you. He wants to take care of Megan. Let him Mom, he's good at what he does, and we know him. Mandy says to tell you she's very sorry and will come over as soon as she can. Nicole is going to drive me down soon. You love you—no wait—that's wrong—I love you."

"Go easy, Gail; although it doesn't seem to matter any more does it?"

"Don't worry about me Mom. I'll see you soon. Bye for now."

I'd always liked Mandy, way back in the sixth grade when she and Gail had first met. She, of all Gail's friends, liked me too, and was never in awe of my "funny" accent. Most of my daughters' friends would stare at me as though I'd come from another planet whenever I spoke. One time Megan brought a girlfriend home and said. "Say something Mom" to which I replied. "I'm not a circus act!"

That remark went down through the high school like a dose of salts.

Mandy and I however, spent hours talking about everything, mainly boyfriends of course; something teenage girls often found difficult sharing with their mothers. She had maturity beyond her years and was a good stabilizing influence on Gail.

When Mandy was only seventeen, it didn't surprise me to hear she was going steady with Scott, a young man training to be a funeral director, and likely to be her husband. He was also a teenager, and the first time I met him I tried to work out why someone so young would choose such a career. It certainly was unusual, but little did I know how much I would lean on and trust him now.

I couldn't sit still, I couldn't stand still, and I had to keep moving. I went outside and again knelt to embrace the dogs. I rested my arm along the soft sun-warmed coat of Thatcher's back, imbedded my fingers under his collar to the silky knuckle behind his ear, closed my eyes and swayed a little, taking a moment's advantage of the numbness in my brain. It didn't last long before automatic tears flushed my eyeballs, temporarily washing away the grittiness of grief before squeezing through weary lids.

The sound of a car door closing brought me back to earth, and there was Ann.

Oh thank God, my rock had arrived. We stood hugging each other for the longest time without the intrusion of speech, words completely superfluous. Minutes passed before either of us looked up, and then with faces wet with tears, we slowly made our way inside.

Chapter Five

The phone was ringing. Giles answered it while he held Ann with his free arm. It was his secretary telling Giles she had managed to get a flight for Helen arriving in Orlando at eleven o'clock tonight. Thank you, God.

The word was out. The telephone didn't stop ringing. Not for a second.

I glanced out of the window to see Laura getting out of her car with a bunch of spring freesias in her hand. Sweet, lovely Laura, another of the steak house employees. Only twenty-one years old, but with the wit and wisdom of someone twice her age, and already on the management path. Megan and Laura had butted heads on many occasions. The stubbornness of youth eventually gave in to conformity or compromise or the ability to see just how stupid they both were. After long grueling shifts, Laura, Ann and I formed a motley trio in the pub, where Laura could down a pint or three before we'd finished one.

Right behind her were Nancy and Tom, friends from the running group. Mid- afternoon, were they not working? They were carrying beer and a box of chicken wings. *Sorry, but I still feel like throwing up.*

Our next-door neighbors suddenly appeared. *How did they know?*

Now, as the kitchen began to fill with people who knew Giles and me but not each other, I found myself taking on the more familiar role of hostess at a party. For the most part, they had no idea what to say to me, and touching or hugging was obviously awkward for some. The men had the excuse of handshaking to forego words and became clannish to gender. By introducing them, I began to make them feel better. It was as though I stood outside myself, like an awake out-of-body experience. Shock had turned me into a strange surrealist, one stress molecule at a time.

In this dream like state I made my way to the telephone; I had to have more information. At the same time I began to dial the Daytona hospital number, I heard a voice; that odd coincidence of picking up the phone before it rings. It was Scott.

"I'm so very, very sorry," he said. "Would you like me to take care of the funeral arrangements? Do you know where Megan is?"

I gulped, —whispered "No" and handed the phone to Giles. I liked Scott and understood his line of business but I couldn't cope with the reality of this terrible truth.

I covered my face with my hands and sobbed, body shaking sobs, great rivers of tears running down my face, forcing their way through my fingers like a bursting dam wall. I was completely out of control.

Instantly Ann was by my side. I turned against the wall into the living room, out of earshot and sight of the people in the kitchen.

"I'm sorry," I kept saying over and over again. "I'm sorry."

"Don't be sorry for tears." Ann told me with an arm around my shoulders. "Here have a fresh handkerchief, and cry all you want."

"I have to find out what happened, and how the three girls are. One of them is in bad shape." I blew my nose and some sort of composure was restored.

I could hear Giles saying thank you and goodbye to Scott. He came around the corner and leaned on the wall. I could see misery all over his face, but still no tears.

Cry! Damn it.

"Megan will be in good hands. I have every faith in Scott's ability to take care of everything."

Why the hell are you so bloody calm and I'm such a mess?

"I really should have spoken to him," I said. "Don't we have to go and identify her? I want to see her—no I don't want to see her—is it really her? Oh my God, tell me this isn't happening." And then after a pause when nobody said anything. "I don't want anyone else touching her, or any of that embalming shit."

"Scott's calling back later on; like I said, he told me he'd take care of everything. Because he knows Megan, I think he wants to spare you the pain of going to Daytona, but you can talk to him later."

I knew I had to accept the awful truth, but still I said. "Maybe it isn't her." And wandered to the picture window to see if Roger was still under the tree.

The wave of despair passed for the moment, so I dialed the number to the hospital again.

"I would like to talk to someone who can give me an update on the three girls admitted today after a car accident on the I 95."

"Just one moment."

Another voice. "Can I help you?"

Again. "Yes, I would like to talk to someone who can give me . . . "

Another voice. "Who's calling please?"

I told them my name and that I was a nurse.

"Are you a relative?"

"No, but . . ."

"I'm sorry, we can only give out medical information to a relative."

"The hell you can't. Listen to me. My daughter was killed in that accident; so was her friend, the one who drove the three girls you have with you down from Ohio. I'm trying to be nice about this, but I'm in agony here. I really NEED to know how those girls are. Are they even alive?" My voice had reached a querulous pitch that someone from the crowd in the kitchen attempted to calm me by putting their hand on my back. I angrily shook them off.

"Just a moment." Shit and double shit, and what seemed like hours later, yet another voice.

"This is the charge nurse speaking, and I can tell you all three girls are alive. One has a concussion, ruptured spleen, and multiple fractures of both legs. She's in the operating room now. Another has bilateral fractured femurs, broken ribs, and multiple contusions. She'll need surgery later in the day. The third has a fractured elbow and minor cuts and bruises to her head," she paused. "I'm very sorry for your loss."

"Thank you," I whispered. "Thank you for your compassion and time taken to speak to me. I—I am also a nurse—I—thank you— my husband. . .we will come to see them soon. Please tell them I called."

Ann was standing close, and I related to her how the surviving girls were faring.

I looked up to see a mass of people. My! How the word had spread so quickly!

Then I overheard someone say word of the accident had been on the local TV station's one o'clock news.

The kitchen counter looked ready for a party, covered with all sorts of food in cardboard containers, plastic plates, cups and napkins. Where on EARTH did that enormous bag of popcorn come from? I was amazed that anyone coming to the house this afternoon would stop to buy anything.

Oh no! Surely my ears were deceiving me. I thought I heard

someone laugh. God forbid! It sounded like Giles, but I did not have the courage to find out; I couldn't cope with coping.

I felt as if choking, and had to make my way through the empty dining room to the quiet of my bedroom. I needed air, space and to be alone—I had to get a grip. But why? Inherent responsibilities to my "guests"? They seemed just fine, much better than I.

I hurt so badly. My bones and muscles ached with this horrid knowledge; my thumping heart fragmented and bleeding. I should have secreted a knife from the kitchen to finish slicing through this pound of flesh. But that would have been the unkindest cut of all, guaranteeing me never to see Megan again. All true believers go straight to God in Heaven amongst the angels, but not if one takes one's own life.

I rinsed my face with cold water, and as I was drying off, looked into the bathroom mirror. An old crone stared back at me with hooded, lifeless eyes, a drooping mouth and disheveled hair. Was this me or my mother? Mum if it is you, help me please, I need you. It was you who died on this day, not Megan.

Oh my God, sweet Jesus, please don't tell me Megan's dead. I suddenly realized that a years' old premonition had come true. For some time I had carried the awful notion that one of my daughters would not celebrate her twenty-first birthday. This frightful forewarning was more than the usual parent thing of worrying about the child every time he or she was not in sight. This was darkness in my soul, a burden to bear of incredible magnitude, which put me in a dead funk every time its shadow crossed my path. I categorically knew one of them would not make it to adulthood.

This was not something I thought about daily however, and over the years, I didn't tell too many people. Maybe one or two really good friends who didn't take me seriously and always managed to placate me with platitudes. Even the occasional trip to the County

Faire psychic did nothing to allay my fears. Would any friend remember those conversations now?

Would I be forever haunted by my own statement:

Megan! One day, you're going to kill yourself driving like that!

Chill, Mom!

The ghastly truth, the dreadful reality was setting in. I stood there staring at myself, and for a short time was completely devoid of thought. Blank brain cells registering nothing, how wonderful.

Behind me, Ann was reflected standing in the doorway.

"I just need a moment on my own," I told her. "I know all those people out there mean well, but I can't face them right now, and I don't know what to do next." The decision was made for me as Giles came through to the bedroom with the phone in his hand. I hadn't heard it ring.

"It's Trevor, the Translife guy."

I automatically accepted the phone from Giles, but with a passing flash of anger—

Why can't you speak to him? Why do I always have to do everything?

Be reasonable. I wouldn't have liked it if Giles hadn't let me speak to Trevor.

All he wanted as it turned out were directions to the house in order for us to sign a consent form.

Please Giles, deal with this, whatever it is.

Where was Gail? I needed to see her, touch her. It was five o'clock already; she shouldn't be that much longer.

I lay down on my bed and closed my eyes. Instantly images of Megan—Megan---

Alive, vibrant, screaming. What happened to you my darling child? Did you die in an instant? Did you cry out for me? I'm so sorry my sweet; hush: I'm beside you always; no harm will come to you now. My beautiful girl, my wonderful baby, my free and loving spirit. We needed no bonding time at your birth. It was there the moment you burst into life, your destiny and mine, living and dying in one breath.

"Gail's here," Ann's gentle voice stirred me.

And there she was, in my arms sobbing, her long dark hair smelling of cigarettes trailing about my face. We stood there for the longest while, unable and unwilling to let go.

"I'm so sorry, Gail. I'm so sorry for not being with you. Let me look at you. Are you OK? Oh dear God, this is so awful. What are we going to do? Thank God you're here."

"I'm OK Mom. I managed to sleep a bit on the way down and feel better for it. Does anyone know what happened?"

"Not yet. Carl—you remember Carl? The police officer friend of Dad's? He's going to call as soon as he can with more information. Scott's on his way to the hospital or wherever Megan is."

"I know," said Gail. "Mandy called me on my cell phone. She's meeting Scott here later. I said she could; I hope that's all right with you."

"Of course. Have you seen the mob in the kitchen? We'd better go out there. Apparently the accident was reported on the midday news, that's how the word has spread so quickly. What about something to eat?"

"No thanks, Mom, just another drink. I don't suppose you've eaten anything either."

I thought back to five thirty this morning and how that cup of tea had sustained me for over twelve hours. I would choke on food right now.

"When's Helen coming? Is Eric coming with her?"

"Tonight at eleven. I haven't heard from Eric yet, and he'll obviously have to get a different flight from Ohio."

Poor Helen. My heart went out to my lovely, capable eldest daughter alone in her grief in Chicago, without the support of her boyfriend Eric. He too would be suffering in Ohio, and both would have to endure a miserable flight alone.

Giles came into the room and as he had overheard my last remark told us that Eric had indeed called and would be here tomorrow. Thank God. He had loved Megan dearly, and would add tremendous comfort not only to Helen, but also to us all.

Ann told us Trevor was in the dining room waiting for us. How appropriate he was sitting in Megan's chair. The mere sight of the poor man started the tears afresh. He was so gentle, so compassionate as we signed the consent forms. He would do what he could and be back in touch with us as soon as possible.

I began pacing again, crying again, struggling to maintain some sort of composure. Why couldn't I let it all go? Nobody teaches us how to mourn. Now I envied the women I'd seen on TV prostrate and hysterical over their loved ones' bodies. There was something about the wailing—the shrieks and strange cries. Were they better bereaved than I?

Anger was on the rise, and I wanted to scream at everyone to get the heck out of my house. Piss off you bloody morons. What are you here for anyway? For show? Go!

Leave me the hell alone.

You can stay Ann. You are the only one with the grace and dignity to keep quiet. Megan, Ann is great. She knows the value of that little expression you hated:

God gives you two ears and one mouth so you can do twice as much listening as talking. A lesson, my darling you never quite mastered.

My decorous upbringing came to the fore. "Manners maketh man" my Mum used to say. Be nice and respect your fellow man.

Yeah! Well explain something to me Mum. I don't understand

why Megan had to die. Maybe this is the one time in my life when I can be totally honest even if it means outrageous behavior. I'm a hypocrite, thinking contemptuous thoughts.

"Thank you for coming" "How kind of you to come" "You're so thoughtful" "That bag of popcorn was just what I needed at a time like this" Jesus!

Thank goodness there was an overriding numbness that stopped me from being openly, bold-faced rude. They were good people, for the most part innocent of death, and certainly naïve in dealing with it. They didn't deserve harsh treatment, so thank you, God, for keeping me silent.

It was dark outside now and many had left or were in the throes of leaving.

I did feel resentment towards Giles who spent so much time talking with friends, avoiding me. What more had to happen to get his undivided attention?

Later.

"Mom, please walk down the hallway with me," said Gail. "I can't do it on my own. I know it's stupid but I can't pass by Megan's room."

Neither can I, but I have to. Why am I always so bloody capable?

I stood up slowly, weariness and lack of food began to take its toll. Arm and arm, Gail and I walked to her bedroom beyond Megan's. Gail's eyes did not waver, but I couldn't help a sideways glance to the familiar photographs and swimming ribbons on one wall of Megan's room, and the trophies standing on the dresser.

Only three months ago, Megan had swum her way to two state championships, knocking seconds off the school records, a feat she quite rightly reveled in.

Proud of her? Proud of her? I hardly knew where to begin to celebrate.

Go, Megan Go! Champion that you are. Can you still hear the roar of the crowd my girl?

I can.

Keep going, put one foot in front of the other—I'll deal with this later.

I went into Helen's room and automatically started to tidy up after the girls from Ohio. Not one of them would ever spend a night with me again. I wondered how the surgeries went. I prayed.

Scott had arrived looking very grim. He pulled Giles and me to one side and hugged me tightly. With tears in his eyes he told us it didn't look good.

"I'm afraid Megan was pretty smashed up," he said. "I honestly believe she must have died instantly."

Oh no, no, no. Once again, I wept and wept, now unable to control myself.

"And Heather?" asked Giles.

"Heather was driving," said Scott. "She too died instantly of apparent massive brain trauma. I'm so very sorry, but I really think neither of them could have known anything about it."

Bugger Heather, she killed my child.

Chapter Six

Giles put a beer in my hand. "Here drink this," he ordered.

OK. I gulped it down, not realizing the effect it would have on my empty stomach. When I stood up I wobbled as good as any drunkard.

"You must have something to eat," said Ann. "I know it must be difficult, but you haven't had anything since this morning, and that's bound to make you weak."

"Sorry, Ann. I can't face food yet. I'll be all right. Look it's getting late and we have to leave for the airport very soon. I don't know what I would have done without you today, but please go home to that wonderful husband of yours and try to get some rest yourself."

"Kenny called me on my cell phone not so long ago. He's very upset. He loves you and loved Megan dearly, but I know him, he won't be able to see you for a while, or at least until he's got his emotions under control. He did tell me to stay with you as long as you would like me to. I think you need the privacy of family now, so I'll go home and come back tomorrow. Is that OK?"

"More than OK. And please thank Kenny for being so generous with your time. Promise me you'll be back early, and if you can't get through on the phone, just come on over. Thank you, Ann. For everything."

We hugged, which brought fresh tears to our eyes. I walked out to Ann's car with her and said goodbye.

What an amazing woman. Ann, who had no children of her own, yet instinctively understood my pain.

It was dark and cool and still with a sky chockfull of stars.

Star! That was Megan's first word. I remembered that bumpy dirt road in Belize. We'd been to a party at some friends' house up in the mountains. Giles was driving our big Ford truck. Helen and Gail were asleep in the back of the cab, but Megan was wide-awake sitting on my lap (no seat belts or baby seats then). She was almost two years old, and had two big sisters to do all her talking up until then. I nuzzled my cheek against hers and pointed to the sky.

"Star," I told her. "Star," I repeated. And out it came STAR!

I later reflected that was about the most stupid thing I could have done--- taught Megan to talk! From that moment on she didn't stop talking, to herself, to an imaginary friend, to strangers, even in her sleep. Babble, babble, babble—on and on—

The notes from teachers came with every report card: 'Megan can be very disruptive in class because of her incessant talking'. What Megan couldn't do was whisper. She would bolt through the garage door into the kitchen as though shot from a canon, yelling all the way. "Mom, I'm late ---Mom, guess what? --- Mom, did you. . . Mom, I'm starving." What she did best was argue, even if she was right. Opinionated? Who? Megan? Ha! She had opinions on opinions.

The dogs sauntered over to be closer to me. I knelt by Thatcher's side, my face close to his. I looked up; star, Thatcher, star.

Giles came outside. "We ought to be leaving for the airport soon. Are you OK?"

Bloody stupid question.

"Yes, I'll make it. I just need to wash my face."

We set off on the forty-minute journey. Gail sat in the back of the car on the edge of her seat, and lopped over the front seats with her chin resting on my left shoulder. She had calmed down, and only I knew she was quite tipsy. She couldn't stop talking.

"What happened to Nicole?" I asked her.

"She's gone back to Jax. She said she didn't want to intrude, but I really think she couldn't handle it."

"Gee, I don't think I even thanked her for bringing you down."

"Don't worry about it, Mom, she won't have noticed. Dad, why did the police call me this morning asking if I was Megan's sister? What's up with that?"

"Yes," said Giles. "That was uncalled for. I think they made a mistake, and I intend to ask Carl about it. To my understanding, the police never notify immediate relatives by phone of a death."

"Will Carl be able to tell us what happened?" asked Gail.

"Yes, most definitely. At least, he'll tell us what the police think happened. By tomorrow we'll know a lot more."

"Where are you staying tonight Dad?"

"I don't know. I hadn't given it much thought."

Oh my God. Was he really going back to his apartment and leaving me on my own.

"Well," said Gail. "I think Mom needs you to be with her." Gail was draped all over me by now and had me in a modified neck lock. Bless her heart; she was looking out for me, doing her best to comfort me, and by osmosis drawing salvation for her.

I couldn't believe it. Giles had to have his daughter tell him how to behave on such a sad occasion. Had the man no feelings? Was ice running through his veins? Was he so utterly, preposterously selfish? Did he want to grieve alone? That's it! This man is so devoid of emotions; he has to escape to be on his own. No one would be allowed to see him cry if he did. God Giles, your mother did a number on you sending you off to boarding school at eight years old. Let someone else be responsible for your sentimental upbringing. Now as an adult, add the British stiff upper lip, don't you know. Stand to a man, and all that. Real men don't cry.

How often had I told him in the past that when we suppress our feelings they come out in other self destructive ways, including anger, rage, drugs or depression to name a few. And how often had he listened to me? No! He was hell bent on accusing me of always being "too emotional". Yeah well, at least I have them; and I'm angry now.

". . . you remember that don't you, Mom?"

"What? Sorry, I was thinking about something else. What do I remember?"

"The Halloween night when Megan and I thought we would scare Helen."

"How could I ever forget?" And began smiling at thought.

"What night was that?" asked Giles. "I don't recall. You'd better remind me, Gail."

"It was so funny," began Gail. "Megan had this idea that if she sat on my shoulders and then draped a white sheet over us both, Helen would be scared out of her skin at the sight of an eight foot ghost coming through her door. We got it all together in the hallway outside Helen's room, and everything was fine until Megan was up on my shoulders and started laughing, which made me laugh, which made her laugh even more. And then I felt something warm and wet trickling down my back. She'd pee'd! We collapsed into a heap, and I swear Mom, I'd never laughed so hard in my life that I almost wet my pants too."

"Me too," said I. "By the time I got to you, all I could see was this white pile of linen, and heard you shouting, "oooogh—oooogh, get off me, Megan". This commotion brought Helen out of her room. She started laughing, which set us all off again. It was hilarious."

"I must have been away on a business trip," said Giles as he wiped his eyes. "I know I wouldn't have forgotten that story if I'd been home."

Tears from laughter now ran down my face, and by the time we arrived at the airport the three of us were hysterically cackling at the images Gail had just presented. What wonderful comic relief to enable us to breathe again.

Still chuckling, we made our way inside the airport to the gate. The usually busy terminal was deserted at that time of night, with only a handful of people waiting to meet the plane. To an outsider we must have looked like a happy family greeting another member. That is until we saw Helen. She was slumped in the middle of the pack, grim faced and obviously exhausted. She threw herself into my arms and Giles and Gail both locked their arms around us. Our depleted family, now four, stood for the longest time in silence, oblivious to anything or anyone else, all of us weeping in our own way, (except Giles, of course).

It was one-thirty by the time we got home. Giles made the inevitable tea and we sat in the kitchen quietly reflecting on the day. Tears were gone now and I took comfort in having my two remaining daughters with me. For a short while, in the solemn, peace of the night, we were the perfect family unit, albeit united in misery.

Now here was an odd happening—Giles and I getting undressed and ready to sleep in the same bed. It had been months since we'd done that, but he'd obviously taken Gail's words to heart. Nothing had been said and I found it all rather awkward in spite of the circumstances. He didn't, and let his clothes fall on the floor where he stood, much as he'd done in the previous twenty-five years. He put his arms around me and kissed me.

"Try and get some sleep," he said. "I'm sure we'll have another equally long day tomorrow."

"Good night."

Before long, I could hear the steady rhythm of his breathing and knew he was asleep. I lay on my back in the half dark and watched the paddles of the over-head fan on their endless rotations. I was so tired, but the instant I closed my eyes I was immediately awake. I didn't trust myself to sleep. I had to stay awake, at least keep one eye open. I had to listen for the Christmas bells I'd hung on the inside of the front door to tinkle, to let me know Megan was home.

Darling, darling girl be safe.

I dozed, and in a couple of hours knew sleep was impossible. It was five o'clock, the time I normally woke. Careful not to disturb Giles, I got out of bed and made my way to the kitchen. I needed a cup of tea. While waiting for the water to boil, I stared out of the window. I loved this time of day—sparrows' fart Giles called it—I don't know if they were, but they were certainly beginning to tune up. A grey mist eerily formed a line six feet above the ground, promising another beautiful spring day in Florida.

The house was quiet. I hoped Helen and Gail were sleeping and I ventured down the hallway to listen to their breathing outside their respective rooms. Yes, all was well.

I took my tea into Megan's room and sat on her bed. I hadn't slept but was rested. My eyes, though swollen, felt clear. A detached numbness had spread throughout my body, and for the time being there were no more tears. The blinds on the window had not been drawn, and in the half-light of dawn I looked around the room. So many memories it was difficult to know where to begin. I inhaled her scent, drew one of her discarded T-shirts up to my nose; I touched the bedspread, automatically smoothing it with the flat of my hand;

my eyes were drawn to the little L shaped tear made by a loose screw
of a suitcase wheel that I hadn't had time to fix.

I noted the pile of clothes off to one corner, and the uncapped
bottle of nail varnish remover and idly thought the contents would
eventually evaporate.

I sat there. I was alive—Megan was dead.

Hush, my child. I'm beside you always and no harm will come
to you now. There is no separation for us. There is no beginning and
no end.

Light came through the window causing the effect of a rising
curtain at a stage play.

Act one: scene one: A mother sits alone on a bed, head drooped,
hands loosely in lap. Dead quiet: The End.

I must have slept through acts two, three and four, must have
missed the roar of the crowd, the hurrahs and "encores" from the
cheap seats and the ensuing exiting comments. "What a brilliant life
she had" "So sad she had to die so young" "Such a shame she. . ."
"If only. . ."

Roger jumped onto the bed, ridding me from this nearly catatonic
state. With tail straight up in the air, he gave me his usual sideways
sweep of a hug, all the while seeking out my hand to pet him.

"Hello Rog," I said as I stroked his head and tickled behind his
ears. "I love you Roger." And the purring got louder.

I stood up and made my way to the kitchen. More tea. This time
I made two cups and took them back to my bedroom. Old habits
were very comforting as I put Giles' cup on the table and got into
bed beside him. He had his back to me, so I played the spoon game
with one of my arms across his body. My fingers fondled his chest
hair as if they had a mind of their own, muscle memory not quite
gone. He stirred, and then turned on his back.

"Good morning," he said in his odd formal way of old. He put his arm around me as I snuggled close. I casually draped my arm across his naked body mindful not to venture too far south. Would I be surprised? Did I want to be surprised? I knew I didn't want to spoil such an indecently erotic moment. Sometimes desire is better than fulfillment. *Thank you, God. He is being sensitive. Wicked, lusty thoughts begone, now is no time for pleasure. And yet I want to be comforted, cosseted and cuddled. I silently screamed out, "Make love to me Giles" I need the oneness of sex. I don't need to be alone right now. Fleeting, futile. I'm sure he would think making love to me at this moment absolutely improper.*

"Tell me it's not true," I said.

"I wish I could. Did you sleep?"

"Not really," I told him. "Dozed a bit and then finally gave up. I've been sitting in Megan's room for the past hour."

Giles moved to sit up to drink his tea. I was sorry the fraction of intimacy was gone.

"What are we going to do today?" I asked.

Golly gosh, that sounded like a question for planning a casual Sunday.

"I want to go to the crash site," said Giles. "But I think we should wait for Carl to call us. I know he was working on it last night."

As if on cue the telephone rang and it was Carl.

I got out of bed and left Giles sitting on the edge talking to him while I took a shower. Abnormal day, normal routine.

I was getting dressed when Helen appeared at the doorway wanting some toothpaste. She looked like hell and obviously hadn't slept very much. She came over and embraced me.

"Are you OK Mom? I'm only just beginning to realize what happened yesterday."

"I'm all right at this particular moment," I told her. "I'll have to take it a minute at a time. What about you? Did you sleep?"

"A little." She climbed on the bed and gave Giles a hug. With his free hand he reached up behind him to caress her head.

"Who's he talking to?" Helen asked me.

"Carl," I said. "You remember him don't you? The crazy policeman who loves motorbikes. He's acting as a liaison between police departments and it's helping us so much. Dad wants to go to the crash site today. What about you?"

"No. I think I'll hang out here and then go to pick Eric up this afternoon."

Giles finished his phone conversation, hung his head for a moment while rubbing both temples. He shook his head, released his fingers and looked up to Helen and me.

"Right. Well, Carl gave me the marker post number on I-95 and he's also arranging for us to go over to meet with the EMTs who were first on the scene. They called for a helicopter for Megan as she was breathing and had a weak pulse. She was unconscious and trapped in the passenger seat on the underside of the upturned car. They got very frustrated when they couldn't get her out and couldn't reach her sufficiently to start an I.V. They cut the roof off the car, and used the jaws-of-life, but it was too late. Apparently she just slipped away."

I stood and stared at Giles dumbfounded. Megan had survived the crash.

I couldn't move. I stood half dressed with my feet bolted to the floor. My heart was thumping clear out of my chest, deafening my ears. My eyes glazed over and I could see nothing. I had returned to the black cardboard cylinder. Safe.

"Mom, are you all right?"
Very clever, Helen that you can talk under water.
"Mom!"

I doggie-paddled to the surface and found myself looking into Helen's eyes. I sat on the bed, cradled my head between my hands and watched the steady drip of tears fall on my bare legs.

"Oh my God. Megan survived the crash." My voice just a whisper.

"Look, we'd better wait to draw any conclusions until after we've spoken to the EMTs," said Giles. "You'll drive yourself crazy with the "what ifs" and "if only-s". Let's just wait till we get a first hand report." Then, in a supreme moment of tenderness he sat beside me on the bed and gathered me up. "I understand it's difficult for you. I know you want to know all the details, so do I, but we'll go after breakfast. I'm going to my apartment now to change, and then I'll come straight back. Do you want to eat here or out somewhere?"

"I don't want to eat at all, anywhere. Please don't be long." I was suddenly defenseless, all capabilities compromised. I felt like a glob of jelly without structure, empty of thought. I needed Giles to be my strength before I became completely stranded in a morass of despair. Was he up to the job?

Giles and Helen left the bedroom together talking in muffled tones. I caught single words like "she" or "look after" and knew they were talking about me. I didn't have the energy to care about being discussed, something I would have bristled over under normal circumstances. But nothing would ever be normal again.

I sat there for the longest time, staring into space, imagining my child mangled beneath a ton of metal. Try as I might to dismiss it, the horrific image played over and over. What were you wearing? Were you asleep? Were your feet up on the dashboard in your usual fashion? Did you scream? Did you try to help Heather? I know you were wearing your seat belt, what happened? And why weren't you driving your own car?

Roger found me again and jumped up on the bed. I swear this

cat understood my pain and was trying in his own way to help. He butted his head against my hand imploring me to stroke him and anyway making it impossible for me to ignore him.

"Rog, Megan's gone. What are we going to do?"

He looked up at me, slanted eyes half closed and smiled.

"Roger, I forgot to feed the dogs last night." I roused myself, put some shoes on and went outside to greet Liza and Thatcher.

"Forgive me you two, you must be starving."

Lolling tongues, wagging tails, they forgave me.

The phone rang two rings before it was silenced. Helen must have picked it up, taken a message and then joined me outside.

"That was Ann," she said. "She's on her way over."

"Thanks darling." A long pause. "Don't you just love these Florida spring mornings?"

Helen stood beside me in the driveway with her arm around my shoulders.

"Mom," she said. "You're the strongest woman I know. We will survive this. We will go on. We need to lean on each other. I'm here for you and love you very much."

Fresh tears poured down my face as I looked at her and nodded.

Giles and Ann arrived in tandem. Ann brought bagels and fruit.

"Ann, it's a weekday, can you afford to take a day off?"

"Don't worry about it," she replied. "I'm not leaving you on your own, and anything I can do to help, helps me through this."

This was a wonderful, successful friendship, accumulated trust on both sides.

The phone rang. Helen answered it.

"Just a moment." I heard her say. She covered the mouthpiece with her hand and told us it was Heather's Dad calling from Ohio. Oh no. I couldn't bear to talk to him now and indicated to Helen to pass the phone to Giles.

"I need to call so many people," I said. "At some point I must tell all our relatives in England, and the longer I leave it the harder it will be."

Snippets of Giles's conversation wafted through to the kitchen. "Yes we were going to Daytona today—yes we had been in contact with Trevor from Translife—so sorry—tragic—help all we can". Silence. Giles came back to the kitchen. "That was tough," he said.

I summoned courage to dial my younger brother's number in England.

"Hello mate," he answered, so cheerful. "How's things?"

"David, there's been a terrible accident—yesterday—Megan and her friends from up north were driving home from the beach—mid-morning—they crashed—Megan's been killed."

"Oh my God, Oh no, Oh God, how awful. How? Jes-sus. Carol, come here quickly."

My sister-in-law's voice was already in a panic when I heard her ask David what was wrong. So I had to repeat the dreadful news once more, a practice run for the many calls I would have to take that day and forever after. David agreed to tell Michael my elder brother. Neither David nor I cared very much for his wife, Angela, and I wasn't about to "be nice" or to accept the string of predictable platitudes she would surely dish out. "She's in the hands of the Lord. God knows best. She's with Jesus. She's in a better place", words I intrinsically knew were true, but at this moment would make me sick.

"'Bye David, no there's nothing else you can do. I'll call you soon. Thanks. 'Bye."

Another call to England, to Giles' brother, Charles, and his wife,

Maggie. No reply, but I couldn't leave such disastrous news on an answering machine, so left a message asking them to call us urgently. I was relieved.

No sooner had I hung up the phone that it rang again. Carl first, Scott with funeral notices for the newspapers to approve, the headmaster from the High School, Megan's numerous friends in rapid succession, colleagues from the Steak House and finally Translife Trevor.

"I'm sorry to tell this," he began. "But I'm afraid we could salvage nothing from Megan's body."

"What? Nothing?"

"I'm so very sorry," he continued. "But it was a very traumatic accident that left her broken. Most of her long bones were fractured, and the chest injury had damaged her ribs and heart. I can only repeat how sorry I am, she must have been in fine living shape, and I know how much you wanted her to contribute to the Translife program."

OK. OK. you don't have to sell me anymore. Get lost.

"Thank you," I said quietly. "Thanks for trying. Goodbye."

This information told me a lot. You poor little brat, you must have bled profusely from all those broken bones, and I imagined the blood pooling in her limbs and body, eventually drowning her.

Chapter Seven

I needed air; I needed to get out of the house, away from the phone.

"Let's go." I said to Giles, and to Helen and Ann. "Let Gail sleep as long as possible, she's not a morning person. Ann, thank you so much for manning the phone. You have Giles' cell number, and we'll be in touch. I don't think we'll be gone too long."

Late March in Florida is absolutely beautiful, not too hot but with plenty of sunshine. We had to make a stop at Giles's office, but I sat in the truck still trying to get myself together after all the shocking early morning news. The ride over to Daytona was quiet, and I was glad Giles had taken the back roads and not the interstate. He talked on his cell phone to Rosa giving her more instructions on how to organize his day at the office. The sun shimmered reflection through the truck's windows and I closed my eyes. With head back and the gentle rhythm of tires on tarmac I was soon dozing as near to sleep as possible without losing total consciousness. I felt a hand on mine: *well, there's a thing.*

"We're almost at the interstate. Do you want to talk a bit about what we're going to do for Megan's funeral?"

"I don't want a funeral," I said. "I don't want one of those nasty viewings either; I couldn't bear to have hundreds of people gawping at her."

"We don't have to. Can we agree to cremation?"

"Definitely."

This was something we'd never thought to discuss; what to do with elderly parents' remains, at a pinch even a brother or sister, yes, but one of your children. There should be a higher law against it. Children are supposed to outlive their parents.

Giles was so good with maps and directions. Immediately on spotting the marker Carl had given him, he looked for a suitable place to pull over on the right-hand verge. It was mid morning, the traffic just a trickle. Giles held my hand, and together we ran across the road to the center median, down the grass slope and into the thicket. It was easy to see. First, I noticed a gash six feet high in a cypress tree trunk and torn limbs strewn about the base. Tire tracks from the emergency vehicles guided us in. Giles was ahead of me but came back to help me over the roots and branches of pine saplings, scrub oaks and palmetto palms destroyed in the crash. The car was gone, the roof still there propped on its side as a jagged canopied reminder of what must have been a desperate fight for life. I stumbled on beer bottles, two full ones and an empty. Chewing gum wrappers, a plastic cup, a lipstick without a top, plus all sorts of stuff and litter obviously thrown from Megan's car on impact.

What amazed me most was that I didn't cry. I gazed around me as though in a trance. It wasn't real; it was a movie set. I had blocked out the sounds of traffic. It was calm, peaceful almost. It was as though Megan's guardian angels were there to shore me up, to protect me from further hurts. She's OK they seemed to say, and it was all right. For just a second I understood

I did however, sense Heather's presence, and unlike the placid composure I'd felt minutes before, here was this child's tormented soul screaming for liberty.

Giles's voice drifted in from a distance, "five eighteen year olds, where do you think they got the beer from?"

"Hell's teeth, don't you know they all have false IDs these days. Oh no, do you think they were drunk at nine o'clock in the morning?"

"Who knows?" said Giles "We'll have to wait for the autopsy reports. I'm sure they will have taken blood samples for alcohol and drug testing."

So controlled, as though we weren't part of this movie—no, not a movie, this awful truth.

"Well, I know Megan drank beer, but not that often because of her swim training, and I'm almost positive she never took drugs because of the random tests done at the meets. I realize she wasn't perfect and I can't speak for the others. Look Giles, I don't know how long you want to stay here, but I'd like to go. I have a definite need to meet with the paramedics. I want to find out if they know what happened. It really bothers me that she survived the crash and they couldn't help her live."

"Right, let's go."

It must have seemed strange for travelers on that stretch of interstate to see two adults appear from the center median bushes and attempt to cross the road to a waiting car. From the highway there was no indication of devastation, no hint of our tragedy.

It was still too much for me to grasp and fully understand. I'd been told Megan was dead. Megan IS dead. Dead, dead, dead. I had to keep saying it to myself, over and over again, but there is a section in the brain that refused to totally accept that this is true. How could this be? What did it mean? Here was a perfectly healthy, vibrant young lady, full of life and promise and in one second all that energy is snuffed out as quickly as a candle flame. It didn't make sense. It couldn't be reasoned.

Actually, I wanted to stay numb. I should have stayed at the crash site. I was at peace there, with Megan forever. I did not want to deal with physical, emotional and geographical issues, mine or anyone else's.

Lack of sleep, extreme stress, I was drifting again, an out of body existence half a level above my own. An extra jolt of the truck bumped me back to the living. We were entering what looked like a used car lot.

"I think this is where the Toyota will have been towed," said Giles. "Carl wasn't too sure. Could be one of two places."

I didn't even know we were going to see the car, and I should have stayed in the truck, but without thinking I found myself following Giles. We entered a grimy, shed like office. I paid little attention to the conversation between Giles and a tall skinny man with long greasy hair and black-rimmed glasses with thick lenses. He was dressed in navy blue overalls: Manager? Salesman? Mechanic?

I found myself trailing behind both of them as we moved between cars in varying stages of disrepair to the back of the lot. However, my attention was fully alerted when I overheard "greasy hair" telling Giles, "Oh yes, she was conscious and talking—saying her legs were trapped and she couldn't move."

What! I was dumb struck. What the hell was going on? First we're told one thing and then another.

". . . they used the jaws of life—tough time—really difficult. . ."

My head was throbbing; I closed my eyes. Help me someone please. Who is this moron talking to Giles? How does he know all this? And then I saw it, the remains of Megan's car, her pride and joy now a crippled shell devoid of roof standing forlornly alone. Both air bags had been deployed and looked grotesque covered with blood in different colors: lively red to decaying brown. I clung to Giles for support at this grisly sight. More tears, a welcome veil. I had to turn away; I couldn't bear to speculate on Megan's fate. I stumbled my way back to the truck and waited for Giles.

Dear oh dear, I must pay more attention. I must not subject myself to this emotional abuse. Dearest Megan, were you conscious or unconscious? Will I ever know for sure? I didn't need to see the car. Giles probably did, to deal with his grief in a masculine spatial, cognitive way, whereas mine was more emotional and spiritual. I understand this, so why did I want him to be like me? Better that both of us didn't succumb to blubber and hysterics.

We were back on the road again.

"None of the tires looked like they were blown."

I said nothing.

"The only part unaffected was the rear view mirror, which seems strange as I would have thought that was the point of impact."

I held my tongue.

"And the seat belt looked like it had been cut. Did you notice the passenger seat was almost up to the dashboard? Megan's legs couldn't possibly have been on the floor."

Shut up, shut up, shut up for Christ's sake, shut up.

"Please Giles, could we not talk about it. I wish I'd never seen it."

"Sorry."

We traveled in silence to the EMT station just a few miles further on.

Giles recognized Carl's motorbike outside the fire station.

"Go ahead," I told Giles. "I need time to compose myself, I'm not in good shape."

"Are you going to be all right?" He caught my eye, a hurried glance. No warmth.

Don't keep asking me that. Of course I'm not all right, and never will be again.

"Just give me a minute."

Giles went into the building alone. Why did I feel so angry? Why was resentment directed toward my husband? Was it because he was coping better than me? I thought back to the lovely but brief moment of intimacy in bed earlier in the morning.

Coddle me some more Giles. Make all this go away.

Within a few minutes, he and Carl came out of the station. I got out of the truck to receive the biggest, bearish hug from Carl, the buttons and buckles of his police uniform indenting my flesh. This was the first time I'd seen him, and he gathered me up as though I weighed a couple of pounds, lifting my feet clear off the ground.

"I'm so sorry, so very sorry; she was such a special girl, so very dear to me."

"Thank you," I said. "And Carl, thank you so much for all your help. What would we have done without you?"

"Don't even think about it. I was glad to be in a position to help, and if you need anything, just let me know. The paramedics who were first on the scene are over in this building and expecting you." He directed us to a small mobile house adjacent to the main structure.

"I'll leave you and Giles to talk to them alone. I'm going back to work and I'll be in touch with you real soon."

"Thanks again, Carl. Come over to the house when you get a chance."

I followed Giles up the three flimsy wooden steps leading to the open doorway of the home away from home office of these incredible people who are first on accident scenes. We met Jeff, a short, middle-aged man, bald as a coot, bushy eyebrows that formed a caterpillar line across his forehead, and with an enormous potbelly.

How can he move quickly or even bend over.

Then there was Janice, a slim young blond who couldn't have been more than twenty-five years old.

Inexperienced? What an odd couple sent to save my daughter.

"Come in, come in, take a seat." Jeff shook Giles's hand and then mine. We were offered drinks, but I couldn't stomach a thing.

Nobody wanted to speak first, and it seemed to me the medical personnel were a wee bit nervous. This was immediately confirmed when Jeff started to speak.

"Uh," he cleared his throat. "First, please accept my condolences for your loss. Um- sorry- but we're not used to seeing relatives after the fact. How can we help you today?"

"We want to know what happened." Giles said.

Short, straight to the point. Giles. My hero.

"We'll have to wait for the official police report," replied Jeff. "It's too early to make any presumptions. All I can tell you is the state of victims at the scene."

"We've heard conflicting stories about Megan," I ventured. "She was the front seat passenger, and we've been told one: that she died instantly, two: that she was alive when you got there, and three: that she was conscious and talking. I need to know the truth, the honest, plain, simple truth, no matter how much it hurts." And then, through muffles sobs, "I just need to know she didn't suffer."

Giles put his arm around me.

"My wife's a nurse," he said. "She wants the details. I'm sure she'll be able to handle it."

"I'm sorry." I said and blew my nose.

Janice was standing off to one side and slightly behind me, but I heard her sniff and then blow her nose too.

Jeff drew his chair up to face me, ever so close.

"I'll tell you now what I know," he said. "When we first arrived, the car was on its side with one of the passengers sitting close by. We quickly ascertained there were broken bones but no life threatening injuries with her. It was obvious nothing could be done for the driver, she was dead. Two back seat females were pinned by their seat belts, (*Look Mom, I make them all wear their belts*) one was conscious, the other wasn't. Both had serious injuries. Our main concern though, was for your daughter trapped in the front. Jesus, that car was overturned, on its side and she was down there at the bottom."

Jeff swallowed a gulp of soda.

Get on with it.

He continued, "She was not conscious, but was shallow breathing and had a very weak pulse. We had a frantic, frustrating situation; we couldn't gain any access to her. No way. I couldn't start an I.V. or even put an oxygen mask on her face. . ."

With head bowed, he covered his face with one hand, thumb and forefinger rubbed his eyes as he slowly shook his head from side to side. Nobody spoke. There was a deathly silence. "I'm so sorry, but—ah—there was nothing we could do." Without looking up he said, "—ah—she just slipped away."

C'mon God, for all that's Holy, don't do this to me. You let her survive only to take her away minutes later. That's not fair.

Life's not fair. Nah, nah nah-nah nah nah.

Dry-eyed, I stared at him. "So she never spoke. Who did?"

"That was the girl immediately behind Megan who kept telling us her legs were trapped."

"OK." said Giles. "We've just been to see the wrecked car, and the man there told us it was Megan who had spoken."

"I'm sorry," said Jeff. "That's not true. And that man had no authority to tell you anything. I apologize for his behavior, and I will be making a full report about this."

I could tell Jeff was back on familiar ground with more confidence in his voice.

"How long, I mean—did it take—how much time did you spend with Megan?"

"About twenty-five minutes before she expired."

Don't you just love that medical word "expired" like some magazine subscription past due.

There was nothing more to be said. I didn't want to hear the gory details. It was done, over. We had the information we came for. I stood up, giving cue to Giles to do the same.

"Thank you. Thank you both for trying. This is awful for us, but now I know she couldn't have known anything about the crash, or suffered, I feel somewhat relieved." And then, "she didn't know, did she?"

"No. I don't believe she did." Jeff said quietly.

"I don't think she did either," volunteered Janice. "I'm sorry we couldn't do more. It's so tragic, especially with someone so young."

This slip of a girl came towards me; I could see hesitancy in her eyes. Not good medical protocol, so I made up her mind for her when I held out my arms and we hugged, a feminine, totally compassionate salute. Silently then, I bounced off Jeff's ample girth as he followed Janice's example, perfunctory by comparison. They both shook Giles' hand and we were gone.

"Take me home please," I ordered. "I can't take any more today."

"Do you want to eat? We could stop somewhere for lunch, or pick up something on the way."

"No," I said. "But I suppose I ought to."

It was well over twenty-four hours since I'd consumed anything but tea, and I was amazed at how steady I felt. Adrenaline, a marvelous freestanding life support system.

"It's all a bloody cock-up," I said to Giles when we were back on the Interstate. "First the police call Gail before they call either of us, then the hospital refuses to talk to me and that dreadful man at the car lot spouting untruths. If we didn't have friends in the right places with inside information, imagine where we'd be now?"

"You're right," said Giles. "I should think that mechanic, or whatever he was, will lose his job. Don't forget though, that the majority of people don't want to know the details, wouldn't visit the crash site or speak with the paramedics."

"I'm glad we went though, aren't you? I feel a little better knowing Megan didn't suffer, but still can't help wondering if they could have pulled her from the car, she might have had a better chance."

"Uh-huh."

We traveled the rest of the way home without a word.

Row, row, row your boat gently down the stream,
Megan Leigh, Megan Leigh, Megan Leigh, Megan Leigh.
Life is but a dream.

Megan as a baby squealing with laughter, being lifted higher and higher on the makeshift seesaw of my crossed leg—over and over. . .

Row, row, row your boat. . .

I was unprepared for the reception when we arrived at the house. We couldn't even park in our own driveway for the mass of cars everywhere. On entering the house, a blast of perfume and noise hit me. The kitchen was a throng of people—talking, eating, sitting, standing. I recognized Karen and Jane and James and Tom among the multitude, all good people, but—I looked around to see bunches and vases and gardens of flowers propped on every surface. Ann spotted me and came over.

"How was it? Are you OK?"

She saw my face; I looked aghast at my surroundings. Food covered the entire kitchen counter; brightly colored coolers were stacked against the wall, the television was blaring and I could hear someone pecking away at a keyboard. On closer inspection into the dining room, I saw one of Giles's running club friends engrossed in his computer. He glanced up and told me he was making a web site for Megan.

Holy mother of God, my home has been invaded. It looks like a damn job site.

"I know," Ann said. "It's overwhelming isn't it? The phone's been ringing off the hook. The local TV station has aired the story, including interviews at the High School with the principal and some of Megan's friends. A few of them came by this morning. I have a list of calls."

"Ann, I don't think I can take this, it's too much. Thank you for being here and answering the phone. Where're Helen and Gail?"

"They've both gone to pick up Eric at the airport. Look, go to your bedroom and lie down for a bit. I'll make you some tea and we'll go over the calls. Have you had anything to eat?"

I hate food; the sight, sound and smell of it. Food is life and I want to die.

The phone list was a yard long; some people I'd never heard of, some I'd quite forgotten and a couple of surprises, one being the cook at the restaurant where Megan had had her first job when she was fifteen. I wondered if he'd bellowed at her for screwing up orders as the last one had done.

Giles told me he had to go to his office, but would be back shortly.

What could be more important at his office than to be with me at this time?

Go! You rotten bastard. Leave me here alone with all these sodding people. Run away, like you usually do whenever there's a crisis. Bloody mouse.

I fought my way to my bedroom. "Hello, I'm glad you're here…" *Be nice.* "Yes thanks, I'm OK. . ." *Piss off.* "No there's nothing I need right now. . ." *Except for you to leave.*

Close the door. Peace. The chaos at the other end of the house was mercifully gone if only for a moment. Now there's a welcome sight curled up asleep in the middle of my bed. Come here Roger, my orange bundle of fur, I need to be stroked; I need the comfort of your fur against my skin. Of course the phone rang again and foolishly I answered it, an automatic reaction.

"This is Julia from The Orlando Sentinel newspaper. I work in the obituary division and was hoping I could talk to you about Megan." She paused, and when there was no response from me quickly went on. "First of all, I'm very sorry for your loss."

"Thank you."

The gentle voice continued. "So many of our obits are of older people done with life and following the natural plan. I've done a little research, and Megan sounded like such a dynamic person that I would love to write a special article about her."

She touched a chord, this person who wrote about death for a living. There was something in her voice that invoked warmth, compassion, interest, but most of all she was giving me an opportunity to tell the world about my child. For the next twenty minutes or so I talked, she listened, as I relived events throughout the life of my wonderful daughter. I told her race times from Megan's first swim meet at the age of six to busting the school records and State championships only three months ago.

Tears of pride trickled down my face as I recounted Coach Tyler's recent post swim season banquet speech. He had told his audience how Megan had been his "ace in the hole". He had known, although a length behind the lead swimmer, that, with her fiercely competitive spirit, Megan would win both relay races as anchor leg. Nobody could touch her; she really smoked 'em. I told my empathetic listener how Megan and I had exchanged a special look, all knowing between mother and daughter, bursting with love, pride and yet with just a smidgen of smugness.

Yes, you did it my girl, you did it.

I stared into space. The telephone conversation minutes before led me to reminisce the events of that wonderful State Meet. Climbing out of the pool, ripping off her cap and goggles after the first race, I could clearly see Megan dancing up and down, fervently hugging her coach and teammates, a flash of black lipstick and red fingernail polish, both worn by all the female swimmers denoting the school colors. And then looking up to the stands where all the parents were on their feet cheering, she waved both arms high in triumphant glory, and a grin to crack her face in half. Calmer now, wearing sweats and sneakers, with her long dark hair still damp, I watched her mount the podium on the highest level to receive the winner's award, a gold medallion on a blue ribbon for her, and a monstrous gilded replica of a swimmer destined to grace the glass cabinet in the trophy room for the High School.

There was a soft knock on my bedroom door, followed immediately by the entrance of Helen, Gail and Eric. The girls flopped down on my bed beside me forming a horizontal sandwich. Eric stood in mute shyness, grasped my hand in both of his and tried to speak.

I looked up at him. "It's OK Eric. I know you loved Megan. I'm just so glad you're here."

Ann poked her head around the door. "Mr. Barnes, the High School principal is here."

I roused the girls. "Come on you two. Help me out now."

"No way," said Gail. "He hated my guts."

"Do you think that matters now?" Bless her heart, Helen so quick to placate. "I'll come with you Mom."

Together, we made our way back to the kitchen to greet this

tower of a man. Mr. Barnes, a noble, black column well over six feet tall, used to dealing with diverse parents and all kinds of teenage drama, was clearly uncomfortable now. It couldn't have helped that his attempt to embrace me fell short of the mark, as the top of my head barely reached his chest, and his hands awkwardly caressed my ears. Quickly he stepped back.

"I'm so sorry. Megan was a very lovely girl."

Oh yeah. You didn't think that last month when you suspended her three days for fighting. A black girl twice Megan's size pushed her off the curb while calling her a white bitch. Rightly or not, Megan had decked her.

"Thank you." Helen and I said in unison.

Mr. Barnes' eyes locked on Helen with instant recognition and relief. Even though she had graduated four years earlier, Helen had been a champion swimmer in her own right and a model student not easily forgotten.

Once again, I found myself in a reverse situation soothing the non-afflicted.

"Thank you for coming," I said to Mr. Barnes. "So kind."

I was tired. The minutes became hours, which blended into one another. People came and went. I spoke to some and ignored others. This wasn't a death-denying group, but they weren't facilitating my grief process. They were fulfilling their own, and I found myself more and more resentful consoling them. For the most part, they weren't aware of cultural differences, nor did they understand my response. When someone dies in England, the home is never bombarded with people. Everyone is much more reserved and will keep a safe distance. After the funeral, maybe a few close friends and family members only are invited back to the bereaved home for tea. Now being English in my home in America, we were nationally separated with individual personality and life experiences poles apart. Mourning is an outward social expression of loss, I couldn't seem to react to most of the people here now in my house, and although I tried to appreciate their presence, I wished they would all go away. It was overwhelming, all too complicated, and I had no energy. To boot, my fair-weather husband had abandoned me.

I became increasingly annoyed with the bastard on the computer who had taken over my dining room as his office. I didn't know why his attempt at memorializing Megan didn't seem as sincere as the newspaper journalist, but he kept pestering me for information and didn't know when to stop…where was Megan born?—how old was she when she started swimming?—her favorite. . .

"NO! I'm not getting pictures to go on the web site, not tonight."

Dear Lord, give me a break.

I was in a vacuum of despair and failed to notice Giles had returned until he came to me with a beer in one hand and a chicken leg in the other. I took the beer but not the leg. Greasy, cold chicken fat was not my idea of comfort food.

Don't be so mean, he is trying.

I hated the fact he was so controlled, and could not rationalize his huge fear of expressing emotion.

"You must eat something," he said. "Can I get you anything else? There's enough food here to feed an army."

"OK Giles thanks. Maybe I'll make a ham sandwich."

I could hear Ann talking on the phone. . ."No, I'm sorry, she's not taking any more calls tonight." Pause. Then to me. "This is Heather's mother from Ohio."

Oh no.

"Ann, tell her I'll take her call on the phone in my bedroom." I needed a few extra seconds to compose myself. One bereaved mother to another, what was I to say? Her child had killed mine, but they were both just as dead.

Cindy and I spent a pathetic few minutes sobbing, commiserating, and not saying much of substance. The bond of motherhood was tangible between us, and I had to be careful not to mention her daughter was the driver. What was the point of blaming Heather? Weren't we both suffering enough? I promised Cindy I would speak to her tomorrow, but both of us were reluctant to say goodbye. Despite our geographical and cultural differences, and with no mutual sense of anticipatory loss, at last, here was someone who truly understood my pain.

I was wiped out. I sat on the edge of my bed and rubbed my eyes.

"You'll get wrinkles doing that." My dead mother's voice echoed in my brain.

"Do you think I care?" I shouted out loud, and then screamed, "Mother! Why is this happening to me? First you and now Megan. And both on the same day of the year. For Christ's sake help me." And dissolved into shoulder hunching, body-wracking heaving sobs so violent they scared me.

This was how Ann found me and instantly gathered me up in her arms. I felt more arms around me and heard Helen whisper, "it's OK Mom, we're all here."

Another set of arms, and Gail's voice, "Just cry Mom."

We stood, a huddle of four, all of us by now crying without shame or dignity, lamenting the loss of treasured lives.

Poor Giles, thrust into a circumstance beyond his capacity. He had entered the bedroom to see grief at its height. How was he going to deal with four women out of control? I had to help him.

"Giles please get rid of all those people out there." I nodded towards the kitchen. "It's time for everyone to go. We all need some rest."

"Right."

And I know he was glad to be gone, to do something. Ann said she had to be going also and promised to be back early tomorrow. Helen and Gail left me to undress for bed. Was Giles going back to his apartment? Quite honestly I didn't care one way or another, but was glad to see him come back to the bedroom obviously prepared to spend the second night with me. This night, however, unlike the previous evening when I'd had strange erotic thoughts that I wanted Giles to make love to me, all I craved was sleep.

Please, dear God, please grant me a few hours of blessed unconsciousness.

Chapter Eight

I woke up singing. An aria remembered from my youth, sung by Joan someone. Australian. What was her name? Such a glorious contralto.

What is life to be without thee? What is life if thou art dead?

What is life, what is life? What is life when thou art dead?

Oh no, please don't let that little ditty run circuits in my head all day long.

Another day, more of the same? I lay awake on my back, hardly breathing, and listened to the birds chirping outside. I wished I were a bird, with only anxious thoughts of where the next worm was coming from. I was too heavy to be a bird, to fly. Grief makes you weighty. Sorrow makes you dull. I wondered if a mother bird despairs at the destruction of the nest or cries at the flight of fledglings. Does she mourn the breaking of an egg?

You have wings now Megan, fly away home.

And Megs, take me with you.

I stayed in my bed for as long as I could before bathroom necessities forced me to get up. I had slept, but I was weak and weary, shocked to see myself in the mirror; puffy eyes, red blotched skin, droopy mouth and sagging shoulders, octogenarians looked better than this. Giles was awake now, and watched me through the bathroom door.

"Good morning, have you had tea?"

"No." I replied. "But I'll make some."

"I'll do it," he offered, getting out of bed. He came towards me and folded me in his arms, a tender, familiar caress of old.

Keep him like this, dear God. I love him so much when he throws me a crumb of affection.

After that, it was effortless for both of us to fall into the ordinary routine of daily living. It was only a matter of course to make tea and breakfast and discuss plans for the day. I was cushioned by the conformity, comforted by my knight, and reveled in the early morning glory of another fabulous spring day in Florida.

And the telephone was silent.

The list of things to do that day got longer as we spoke. We had to make a trip back to Daytona and visit the three surviving girls in hospital, not a mission I relished. I knew they were on the third floor, but I also knew Megan was there too, not on that level, but probably below ground somewhere, and there were no visiting rights for her.

We had to connect with Scott at the funeral home. He would know where Megan was, if the autopsy had been done, and when we could see her. I also wanted to reiterate my adamant views on embalming. Nobody but Scott was to touch her and even then minimally.

Don't go putting that nasty stuff into her perfect body.

We had to meet with the pastor at Megan's church to arrange a memorial service. Again, adamant opinions. I was vigorously opposed to either a viewing or a funeral. Here was another cultural difference. There are no public viewings in England, unless you are royalty, and even then the casket is closed. I abhorred the ritual of staring at a lifeless dearly departed, often not remotely resembling his former existence. I did not want to insult my American friends, but to me, there were other ways of showing respect. Nobody was going to gawk at Megan.

There were a million things to do and I had no resolve for any of it. I wanted to stay in Giles's loving embrace, warm and safe, devoid of thought, mindless of decisions. Or, I could have been just as content to sit in my bedroom and gaze out of the window fancifully oblivious of creation.

The telephone rang (of course). It was Ann telling us she was on her way over. What would I do without such a dear friend?

Giles and I continued with the agony of making necessary arrangements to put our daughter to rest. But we were in sync now, lovingly exploring all the possibilities for a becoming farewell ceremony. What would Megan have wanted? What did we want? Did we have to succumb to American ideals just because we lived here? When? Where?

Eric came into the kitchen looking the worst for wear in disheveled shorts and T-shirt, which I recognized from the night before.

" Sorry, but I had too much to drink last night—couldn't sleep— sorry—how are you? —Sorry—damn stupid question."

The magical bubble had burst; back to reality. SHIT.

Don't start getting angry so early in the day—stay calm—you've a long way to go.

"We're OK, Eric," I said. "Would you like some coffee or breakfast?"

"Not right now thanks, I'll wait for Helen. What's the plan today?"

"As soon as my friend, Ann, comes, we're off to Daytona to visit the three girls in hospital, and then on to see the pastor, and hopefully to meet up with Scott and a thousand more things. What about you?"

"No clue yet. It depends on what Helen wants to do."

"One thing you can do for me though Eric, is to ask both Helen and Gail what special music Megan liked. I've an idea for a memorial service."

"No problem. Will do."

On the way to Daytona I formed an outline in my mind of what I wanted for Megan's memorial.

"Giles, I don't want a formal service for Megan. She's going to be cremated, right?"

"I thought that's what we agreed to." He took his right hand off the steering wheel and grasped mine, gently caressing my fingers. *I love it, don't stop.*

"Well, there's not going to be a coffin there, so what do you think of having like an upbeat sort of thing — more a celebration of her life, with maybe by a few prayers? You know how spiritual she was."

"OK, sounds good to me. Did you have anything else in mind?"

"I thought we could all say a few words about her, a snapshot eulogy if you like. I don't know if the kids will agree, but I bet Eric would. How about a slide show?"

"Great. Why not?"

With that, I was silent the rest of the way to Daytona while I formed the makings of my speech.

Nice idea, but would I be strong enough to do it?

All hospitals smell the same, a mixture of carbolic and institutional cooking. This one was no different, but I noticed it was cleaner, lighter and airier than most. We made our way to the third floor nurses' station. All three girls were in the same room, and it was apparent every relative had come down from Ohio for each one. A woman in a white pantsuit and white high heel shoes (*never wear white shoes, my mother had told me, they look tarty*) stood with her back to us. The mass of long, black, curly hair was striking. And then she turned, oh my what a shock. She was old; must have been a grandmother to one of the girls judging from the many wrinkles lining her face, and oh dear, the bright red lipstick was very out of place, literally, and the blue eye-shadow and heavy mascara worthy of theater make-up. This woman had taken center stage in a corridor jam-packed with people. As we advanced, grandma looked me up and down, quickly considered me unworthy of more consideration, and continued her spouting.

Bloody cheek. Doesn't she know who I am? And who is she?

There they were, Jennifer and Julie in their beds with broken legs strung up to the ceiling on traction resembling scaffolding, and Sarah sitting in a chair nearby with one arm in a cast from shoulder to wrist bent at the elbow with protruding supporting rods. What struck me first were their faces: all of them had massive bruises, black eyes revealing sadness and pain. Fresh tears poured down my face as I leaned to embrace each in turn.

"I'm so sorry." "I'm so sorry." "I'm so sorry."

Sorry—pity, sorry—compassion, sorry—mercy, sorry—sympathy. Pitiful.

Nobody could say anything more than that. It was embarrassing for us all. These young girls had just been through a horrific experience, physically banged up, those wounds would heal, but with two friends dead, I was sure the psychological scars would remain forever.

Jennifer introduced me to her mother.

"This is Megan's Mom."

"Hello." I bit my lip. I couldn't think of anything to say.

Dammit, your child is alive and mine is dead.

"This has been a terrible thing for all of us," said Jennifer's Mom.

"I can't begin to know how you feel. To say I'm sorry is not adequate. Is there anything we can do to help?"

I shook my head no, not trusting myself to speak.

Giles was standing to one side of me.

"Eventually," he said. "We'll have to arrange for you to pick up Jennifer's stuff at the house, and perhaps you could help us make arrangements to get Heather's car back to Ohio."

"Yes," chimed in Jenny's Dad. "We're good friends with Heather's parents. We'd be glad to help in any way we can. We'll be here for quite a while yet. Give us your home telephone number and we'll hook up later."

I left the two dads talking and turned back to Jennifer.

"Forgive me asking," I said. "But have you any idea what happened?"

"No," she replied. "We were all asleep in the back of the car. I think Megan must have been too."

"Why wasn't she driving?" I asked.

"After breakfast, Megan said she was too tired to drive. We'd been up most of the night and hadn't got much sleep. One of Megan's friends had had a birthday party in a hotel with a whole bunch of other friends. Heather said she'd had coffee, so she could drive."

Dearie me, responsible Megan to the end.

Jennifer continued, "I asked Heather if she needed company up front, but she said no, she'd be fine. Megan said she would navigate, as Heather didn't know the way back. We were all so tired. . ." her voice trailed off—sorry. . ." Her eyelids drooped, she was almost asleep now.

"We'd better let her rest," said Jennifer's Mom turning to her daughter.

It slowly dawned on me what this child had said. I wanted to vomit with the realization of those words.

If Megan had let Jennifer sit up front with her best friend Heather,
Megan would be alive today and Jennifer would be dead.
NOOOOOOOOOOOOOOOOOOOOOOOOOOOO!

I scanned the room. Julie and Sarah were engrossed with their families. Suddenly I couldn't breathe. I didn't belong here; I had to get out, but not so fast.

By chance, amongst the throng of people was a young woman in her mid thirties, who, I was told was an eyewitness to the crash. Although she said she was quite a way behind Megan's car, she saw nothing untoward with the driving conditions of the day. No tire had blown out; nothing made her suspicious something could be wrong. There were hardly any cars traveling on the interstate at that time of the morning, and everyone seemed to be keeping to the speed limit of 70mph. or just over. She said there were no brake lights, no skidding, that the car just disappeared off to the left, down the grass verge and into the center median. She had stopped, could see the car had come to a violent end up against a tree, called 911, and waited until the ambulance arrived. And now this Good Samaritan was here at the hospital checking on the survivors. *Wow.*

"I'm the mother of one of the girls who died. What happened? Please tell me what happened?" I was close to this petite, well-dressed woman now, imploring. I asked the same questions she'd just given the answers to, and then asked her again, getting the exact same answers. I was making a fool of myself; I couldn't seem to help it.

Get the hell out of here while you've got a scrap of dignity.

We left, and no one noticed.

"The only conclusion that makes any sense to me is that Heather must have gone to sleep." I finally broke the silence when Giles and I were on our way back to Orlando and the next meeting with the pastor.

"Unless she was drunk."

"I can't believe that," I added. "But we'll have to wait and see."

I mulled over the fact that Megan had been the front seat passenger. She had undoubtedly saved the life of Jennifer, sitting directly behind her. I obsessed about this, over and over again. If only. . .

Please God, give me the strength to bear this pain.

Chapter Nine

We were made to wait in the anteroom to Pastor Kevin's office. His secretary, neatly ensconced behind her desk, told us he shouldn't be long. This gave me time to reflect on my own relationship with God, and to conciliate my guilty feelings. This church of Megan's was huge, with thousands of parishioners. It was like a small village with its own cafeteria, little league teams and police traffic personnel. On a Sunday when church was emptying, nobody traveled on that road at midday.

Megan loved it and had belonged to all the youth and Bible study groups, often traveling great distances for weekend retreats. On several occasions she'd asked me to join her for the Sunday morning service and each time I refused, telling her that I was quite happy with my own church and that hers was far too large for my liking.

Why didn't I go with her? Just once?

We'd sent Megan to a private Christian school for the middle school years, 6-8th grade, and I'd always thought they'd done a number on her there, going overboard with the indoctrination to spiritual life. Proof came when more than once I'd caught Megan asking comparative strangers if they'd been "saved".

"Megan," I told her. "Being "saved" only means accepting Jesus Christ into your heart. It's a highly personal thing, and some people might not want to be asked, or might not want to answer you."

Defiant Megan. "That's stupid; it's only a simple question."

I was extremely pleased that she did read the Bible, and turned to her church peers for help and guidance through her troubled teen years, but erroneously thought if I downplayed the churching a bit, Megan might not turn into a holy roller. Forgive me, God and Megan, for I think you both knew her destiny. Both were looking for my assistance. I failed.

Oh no! Don't you go feeling sorry for yourself now with these bloody maudlin thoughts.

A handsome young man burst through the door.

"I'm so sorry to keep you waiting, I'm Pastor Kevin, come in, come in."

A handshake for Giles and me and he led us into his spacious office and directed us to sit on a well-worn but comfortable couch.

How clever, so thoughtful, boxes of tissues everywhere. He's obviously done this before.

He was a good-looking man; sharp, penetrating unusual turquoise blue eyes, beautiful dark wavy hair, clear complexion with a short beard, neatly trimmed. And obvious energy. I liked him immediately.

"This is a terrible time for you," he began. "I'm so sorry; Megan was a wonderful girl."

For the next hour we talked; round and round we went. Why? Why? Why? Kevin didn't have any answers for us. *But why not? Didn't he have a direct line?* Only God knew why—God decides the time, place and manner of testing—this is a test of your faith. *Is there a bigger one?* –God is love. *He has a weird way of showing it*—in time we would know—it's not for us to reason—let's hope she's in a better place—

Is death the end of you Megan?

"Megan had wonderful faith," Kevin said, "You must now put your trust in her."

Yeah, right. That's easier said than done.

"It's OK for you to be angry," he continued. "God understands. He knows your pain; He knows you are in darkness and despair."

"So what have I done to piss Him off—whoops—sorry. What I mean is, why is He punishing me like this? Was I not a good enough mother? How did I fail Megan?"

"You did not fail Megan, and I'm sure you were a marvelous mother. It's pretty obvious you loved her very much. She was always telling me how much she loved you, and all the kind things you did for her."

"I feel so guilty I didn't come to this church with her, not even once."

I told Kevin how much I liked going to my own smaller Episcopalian church. "I let her down."

"It's very difficult not to feel guilty about something or other," he said. "But I'm sure Megan was pleased that you went to church at all, and it's obvious you set a terrific spiritual example for her."

"Someone had to." I looked at Giles, gloomy in his silence beside me.

Say something. You've been just great today, and now I'm disappointed again.

Nearing the end of our conversation, one thing Kevin told us was that in circumstances like these, to look to the heavens and imagine a patchwork quilt stretched across the sky. Underneath while looking up, all one could see were the knots and jumble of crossed threads of an unfinished work, but once we were raised above it, all was revealed as a beautiful masterpiece, and Megan had filled one square. Of course, after that I'd bawled like a baby.

I was on the fringe of hysterics, and it took me a while to compose myself. Apart from the quilt story, nothing Kevin had said made me feel any better. Not to blame him, but he'd made it worse. I'd had to examine my own beliefs, dig deep into the inner chasms of my soul and question my own mortality. He'd given me no plausible answer, only one moment of comfort in his efforts to placate me. No reason to believe in God anymore. And, dammit, I'd spewed forth my guilty feelings, my own convictions of shame and neglect towards Megan. I'd puked it all to a stranger. Was it stupid of me to expect he would somehow make it right?

And yet I did relate to the patchwork quilt. How did this man know I was a seamstress who sewed, and knitted, and crocheted and yes, quilted? Did he know Megan was following in her great-grandmother's footsteps? Did he realize that she was emulating generations of needle-women and was well on her way to being as equally proficient with that needle as I?

"Start it for me, Mom." A six-year old's voice, now a ghost of the past, brought vivid images of the three-inch wide, snake long "scarf" that was Megan's first attempt at knitting.

Damn! What wasted talent.

I became vaguely aware of Giles and Kevin talking. I caught odd words and realized arrangements were being made for the service.

". . . the annex building holds two hundred and fifty people, at six-thirty pm. Call me with any changes. Let's finish with a prayer."

I bowed my head and clasped my hands together, an automatic reaction.

"Dear Lord, at this time of extreme sorrow we commend the soul of Megan to your tender loving care that she may have everlasting life. Shine your light forth on these grieving parents and grant them peace and understanding. Merciful God, hear our prayer, Amen."

I see you; you're right on the edge of the celestial quilt. But I can't quite make out what color you are. Phantom white? Image grey?

"Thank you and goodbye."

"God bless you."

Walking to the car.

"Giles, why didn't you say anything to Kevin? I seemed to be doing all the talking."

"Well, I don't know what you think, but I couldn't stand all that sanctimonious drivel, all that molly-coddling. I've heard it all before and it leaves me cold."

It would.

"Please. How many times have we done this? I've been married to you for twenty-five years and don't recall another occasion like this."

"You know what I mean. I'm sure he churns out that unctuous shit to everyone. As for that patchwork quilt bit, I thought I was going to throw up."

I was shocked.

"I thought that was the best. I don't understand you sometimes, Giles. Your father was a missionary in Africa, a man of the cloth. Brought up within the church family, you must know Kevin was doing his best. Don't you have any holy cells left?"

"No, my brother took over the family business." Giles's mouth was set in a grim downward curve, and I noticed his grip on the steering wheel tighten.

Don't get into an argument about religion at this point. Let it go. He's obviously battling his own demons, but I've never heard him so cynical.

However, the atmosphere had changed. Giles wasn't my hero anymore, we were out of sync, and I was back on the eggshell path. I sulked all the way home.

Christ, I needed support. Where are my lovely girls?

Ann greeted me at the door with the phone in her hand.

"Good timing. It's Scott, he's already called twice."

I took the phone. "Hello Scott. What news?"

"Hey, how are you? I finally had Megan released from the hospital in Daytona and she's here at the downtown funeral home. Don't worry, we are abiding by your wishes, minimal action and no embalming, but she is pretty beaten up. Can I have your permission to make her look as good as I can for you to see her?"

"Yes, but I think you understand I don't want gobs of make-up. I'd rather have the cuts and bruises than something false."

"Trust me, OK? Would you like to come tomorrow?"

"I suppose so Scott. Sorry—but I've had a helluva morning—I don't mean to sound so distracted. Thank you, you've been so good to us. Yes--What time tomorrow? Right. Oh Scott, one more thing please, could you cover Megan's face with a sheet before we go in. I want to be the one to uncover her."

"No problem. Come at nine. Oh and, do you have a date for the funeral yet?"

"Yes, next Monday at six-thirty pm." I gave him directions to the church and Kevin's name and telephone number.

"Leave it to me," said Scott. "I'll make all the arrangements and put a notice in the newspaper."

"You do know that we don't want Megan to be there. No coffin. It's going to be a memorial service."

"Let's talk about that tomorrow. I've lots of options for you and we can decide on format, cards, et cetera. And your wishes for the cremation. Hold on, stay strong, I'll help you get through this."

"Bless you Scott; you've been so good to us. I still can't believe it's happening."

I put the phone down and stood looking out of the window. Thatcher and Liza were playing on the grass, two sets of teeth around one old bone, a united mass of black, white and brown hair, a tangle of tails and legs. I stared at them, they were so happy. They were mindless of evil doing, pestilence or famine. Hunger and poverty meant nothing to them, or even a mild dog skirmish in the next street. So simple. Did they know what death meant? How would I know if Liza missed Thatcher if he died?

My face was wet; I hadn't realized I was weeping. Tomorrow I would see my child for the last time.

In this lifetime.

Chapter Ten

The house was full again. It was as though I'd skipped twenty-four hours and the same people had taken up the same positions as the day before. There was the Computer Bastard typing away, here were friends from the running group partying, and in the background I could hear the TV. It was an out-of-death experience, pun intended.

Send me home please, oh I forgot, this is my home.

I took in a deep breath and let out an audible sigh. *Keep going.*

Gail came up to me, "How are you doing Mom? Where've you been?" Behind her, I made out some of her friends from high school, Shannon and Kelly and that delightful beauty whose name I never could remember. With three daughters in the same high school at once, my house was always filled with friends both male and female, overlapping friends that I was constantly confused as to who belonged to whom. I was glad to see they showed support for Gail and respect for me.

I recounted the day to Gail, but left out the details of our visit to Kevin. Gail was the agnostic one in the family and I wasn't about to raise the delicate issue of religion at this time. I was pleased to see that she seemed calmer, her face free of the strain of the past forty-eight hours. She had a beer in her hand.

"Find me one of those please darling," I indicated. "I feel like getting out of my mind drunk. Where're Helen and Eric?"

"They've gone to see Matt Cooper's family."

I raised my eyebrows in a question. Matt was an ex-boyfriend of Helen's, and briefly also of Gail's, but he reached the end of the line with the youngest sister. He was brought up short when Megan told him, "OK, Matt, three strikes and you're out." How that kid had continued to hang around was beyond me, but he proved to be an invaluable friend to them all.

I took my beer and drifted into the dining room. Giles standing over Computer Bastard, looked up.

"Have you seen this? This web site for Megan? It's great."

I shook my head no.

CB beckoned me over. Why did I dislike this guy so much? He was doing something generous and constructive by creating a biographical tribute to Megan. Was it because he was scruffy; mouse brown hair tied in a loose ponytail, disheveled shirt, cut off jeans and flip flops. He peered at me through John Lennon glasses.

"I need some photos of Megan to complete the job."

*Need. Need. **You** don't **need** anything.* I bristled with indignation but decided to cut him short.

"Fine. I'll fetch the albums and you can help yourself." I couldn't be bothered, let Giles help him.

I finished my beer and had another, aimlessly wandering through the house which was rapidly filling with more people. A crowd of humanity and I'd never felt so alone, utterly isolated, dejected, robotic. I glanced at the list of callers and tossed it aside. I wasn't going to return any calls today. I was so tired of making other people feel good.

Helen had returned and was by my side.

"How are you doing Mom?" Her arms were around me giving me precious comfort, the kind I was craving from my husband and rarely got. "There was a huge piece on the TV lunchtime news about Megan, photographs, swim times and interviews with some of her class mates. It was nicely done. They've even put the flag at school at half-mast for a week. Mr. Barnes spoke too. He said Megan was one of his best students with a very bright future."

"What else could he say? That he was glad she was gone, that her behavior was despicable, and she was one of his worst students ever." Suddenly I became irrationally angry, and lashed out at the nearest object, an innocent vase of flowers. I arm swept it off the table with a single stroke. The glass bounced but didn't break. Water spilled into a puddle that slowly spread over the floor. Jumping on the flowers, I mashed them down with my heels until petals and ferns disconnected from stems and the stems became nothing but mush, little green bits of vegetation that I viciously ground into the now soggy channels of the carpet.

"God, Helen. What the hell has happened to us?"

Soothing Helen had the grace and sense not to say anything, but went to fetch paper towel to clean up the mess I'd made.

Another beer, that's what I needed, I should calm down. Now I had a guilty conscience, those lovely roses and freesias, what a shame, and I hadn't even read the card. I didn't even know who they were from.

Oh, thank God, I spotted Laura getting out of her car, picked up two beers, one for her and another for me, and went to greet her. On the way out I yelled to Ann. "Laura's here, Ann, grab a beer and meet us in my bedroom. I need to talk to the two of you."

The alcohol was performing well. It was like old times, the familiar trio in the pub after a long shift at the restaurant. Only this time, Laura was sprawled over my bed while Ann and I squeezed together on the boudoir chair in the corner. I even laughed.

Nancy ventured in and stood propped against the door frame. Nancy, what-a-messed-up-hypochondriacal (hiccup) boring, woe-is-me individual. Nancy, avoid her if you can because she'll pin back your ears for hours with wretched medical histories. Nancy, stick thin, arms and legs like dangling threads, long straggly blond hair that always looked unwashed, stood before us like a lamb led to slaughter.

"I'm so depressed," she started. "My Mom's so sick and only has a few months to live, and my Dad's driving me crazy, he's so demanding, and Ray (her long-suffering husband) doesn't help, he's never home, (*I wonder why*) my sister couldn't care less, I'm not well myself, I've got this rash and I can't sleep—I want to kill myself."

"OK," said Laura, who'd never met Nancy before. "We can help you with that."

"Yeah," chimed in Ann who'd also never set eyes on Nancy. "We'll finish you off!"

"What's this?" said I. "She can join Megan. Maybe we can strike a deal at the funeral home, two for the price of one."

And with that the three of us collapsed into hysterical laughter.

Poor Nancy, not knowing quite what to make of us, gave a nervous little giggle and left.

"What a nerve," said Laura after we'd stopped cackling. "Fancy coming here at a time like this with all her problems."

"That's Nancy for you," I replied. "I'll make her chief mourner at the memorial service, that'll cheer her up."

"No way," said Ann. "Don't you dare do such a thing."

"Ann, I'm joking."

Giles interrupted our little coven on his way to the bathroom. He frowned as he surveyed the scene.

"I can't think why you three are so hysterical."

I stared at him in surprise, brought up with a jolt.

"But that's just it, Giles. We are hysterical and drunk and so God-damned miserable, and tired and hopeless, and everything's wrong and bloody Nancy was just here with her sob stories enough to make you throw up, and—and—oh shit—don't you ever fault me for laughing." And I burst into tears.

I stood up and shouted at his back as he disappeared into the bathroom, "Don't you put me on a guilt trip, at least I have feelings."

Megan loved to laugh. I know she wouldn't mind if I laughed now.

Sensing my increasing anger, Ann was beside me attempting to lead me back to the chair. I shook her off and stood panting against the doorframe.

"Bloody moron." I muttered.

I heard the loo flush and Giles was in my face, his hand gripped tightly on my forearm.

"Get a hold of yourself," he hissed. "And don't drink any more."

He was gone and I was openly crying, but now I didn't know why. For Megan? For me? For Nancy? For the world? I was drunk and angry but worse, I knew Giles was right. Godammit. Thank God I was in the sanctity of my bedroom with only my dearest friends as witnesses. I ranted a while longer, more to save face than anything else, and eventually calmed down.

"I'd better be going," said Laura. "I was supposed to have had a hot date tonight, but I don't feel like keeping it."

"I'm sorry," I said. "I didn't mean to spoil your evening. I really appreciate you coming over. Are you all right to drive?"

"Sure I am. And don't you worry about me. I'm not sure about this guy anyway. Too needy, lots of baggage."

The three of us moved outside. Ann and I said our goodbyes to Laura.

"Sorry," I said to Ann. "I did rather make a fool of myself tonight didn't I?"

"Nah, who cares? Laura and I certainly don't."

We strolled back inside and I spotted Giles with his arm casually draped over the shoulders of a female runner. They had their backs to me but something must have alerted her. Paula. Yes, that's right, an artsy type with an ugly hooked nose and enormous frizzy hair, who never missed an opportunity to remind us she was from a very wealthy New York family. Really? She must have sensed my eyes boring into her because she turned and seeing me immediately broke free from Giles. He looked at her and then behind him at me, and continued talking to the small group gathered around them. My heart, my poor old heart that had taken such a beating in the last couple of days, lurched to my throat leaving me with the sickest feeling yet. What the hell was going on? Giles—Paula? Surely I must be wrong. Not her.

Gail and her friends sidetracked me. "Three-strikes-and-you're-out Matt" was grinning foolishly. Everyone was drinking too much. I glanced to one side and noticed Giles and Paula at opposite ends of the room. People were coming and going, inside and out. Someone had lit a bonfire in the pit at the end of the garden where several had gathered. This included the dogs, who were obviously enjoying the extra attention and the odd chicken leg thrown their way. It was useless telling anyone not to give them people-food tonight.

Ann went home; she had to be tired, it had been a long day.

Taking another beer from a cooler I wandered aimlessly outdoors, this time around the dark side of the house, away from the crowd. I could still see people moving within, and the fire's blaze out yonder. Well, bugger me; there they are again, Giles and Paula, not touching, but with heads mighty close.

Oh my God, I can't deal with this on top of everything else.

I sat down and leant against the old cypress tree, vaguely aware that all sorts of creepy crawlies could visit me.

Worms crawl in and worms crawl out...itsy bitsy spider...twinkle twinkle little star how I wonder what you are...or is it where you are. . .When sorrows come, they come not single spies. But in battalions. Hamlet or Richard 11, I can't remember. Stupid Shakespeare. Row, row—Megan Leigh Megan Leigh, I love you. . .

"Mom! What on earth are you doing out here?" It was Helen. "I've been looking everywhere for you."

"Hello darling. Come and join me, the ground is lovely."

"Mom, I do believe you're drunk."

I grinned. "No question about it, and I want to stay this way for ever and ever and ever and ever and..."

"I don't think you should drink any more tonight." Helen grasped my hands and pulled me to my feet. "You probably haven't eaten anything and all this booze is going to your head."

I started singing, "I think I'm going out of my head—I think I'm going out of my head over you- ou- ou. You want me, I want you— Hey, look, Helen, there's your Dad with Princess Paula. What do you think about that?"

"Nothing Mom. She's just another runner, nothing for you to worry about."

"Who said I was worried. But if you think I should be..."

"Come on Mom, I think you should go to bed."

She steered me around the house and into the kitchen and wouldn't you just know there they were, together AGAIN, helping themselves from the countless plates of food strewn on the tables. They looked up, but neither said anything or even acknowledged me. Helen quickly came between them and me and virtually shoved me out the door with a passing shot. "Mom's going to bed."

I was glad to be horizontal, arms at my side, eyes closed and relaxed. Beer is good for you, full of vitamin B, great for breast milk. I was drifting, drifting—*shut up will you, whoever is laughing out there, will they please stop.* Giles was right outside the bedroom window talking to two of his buddies. Where was Miss Paula? Now they knew I was removed from the scene they would be free to carry on regardless.

Go to sleep my baby. Close your pretty eyes.

There was a bump on the bed. I stirred, not fully awake, realized Giles had come to bed and was sitting on the edge taking his shoes off. Somewhere in the deep, dark recesses of my brain I registered surprise. I turned my back on him and went back to sleep.

Chapter Eleven

I was operating a video camera but I wasn't weightless. Megan on the other hand was swimming towards me in a zero gravity space capsule. She was barefoot but fully dressed in jeans and T-shirt, her hair free from restraints. Over and over again she "swam" towards me until her face was distorted by proximity, her big brown eyes like liquid chocolate, her long beautiful hair flying in all directions.

"Look at me, Mom, I'm OK. This is great."

Laughing, crazy with excitement, she tumbled lap after lap in that closed small environment.

A hand touched mine, I opened my eyes.

"Good morning, how are you?"

"Fine," I lied. Giles was sitting on my side of the bed drinking a cup of tea. I scanned his face for any indication of rapprochement. There was none. Physically I would be cured with tea and a hot shower but the mental anguish required more effort. I was so ashamed of myself. How could I have behaved so badly?

"Had a little too much beer last night, eh?" I could sense a hint of a twinkle in his eyes, and certainly no disapproval. Maybe he'd had one too many himself. Relieved, I sat up and took the cup Giles offered me.

"I'm sorry. It did get away from me a bit; I should have had something to eat and I would have been fine."

Boy oh boy was I ever lucky. The last thing needed at this time was a full-scale row over petty jealousies.

"We have a difficult day ahead. What time do we have to be there?"

"Nine-thirty." I told him.

We had an appointment at the funeral home for a family only viewing.

"I'll call Scott ahead of time to let him know we're on our way. Gail doesn't want to go. She doesn't want to see Megan in the state she's in. Do you think I'm right by insisting she does?"

"Well," said Giles. "Gail's old enough to make her own decisions. My advice would be to say nothing and just let her tag along. I'm sure she'll go in if Helen does."

"OK fair enough. One last thing Giles, about last night—*Don't! You bloody fool, just let it be*—I did get a bit upset with all those people partying outside, some of whom I've never seen before. I can't believe they knew Megan either. It seemed they were just here for the beer. And I didn't like Paula following you around like a damn puppy dog."

"She's just a good friend trying to be sympathetic. You have your friends and I have mine."

"Yes, well, all my friends are female and it seems yours are too."

Miouw. Sod it, I had said my piece.

Giles didn't reply and left the bedroom. Now I knew I'd been right about those two. There was something going on.

Lordy, Lordy what was that about single sorrows? I must dismiss this from my mind and deal with it later, or it's going to eat me up as surely as any cancer. But how?

Then images from the dream showered my vision. Megan had come to me in the night, bless her heart. She had told me she was OK and I rejoiced in knowing this was true.

She was OK. She was OK.

I expected to see the house in a dreadful state after last night's activities, but was pleasantly surprised. It wasn't immaculate by my standards, but all the food had been put away and all clutter and trash neatly disposed of. Gail, Helen and Eric were sitting at the kitchen counter.

"Hi Mom," said Helen. "Did you sleep?"

"Yes thanks. I'm fine." I replied, forestalling her next inevitable question. "Did you clean up the house?"

"We all did."

"Thanks." I gave Helen and Eric a brief pat and crossed the room to embrace Gail. "I love you all so much." Tears overflowed my lower lids as I looked at the three of them utterly dejected in their own grief, and desperately seeking a way to ease mine.

"I had a dream last night about Megan," I began.

"So did I," said Helen.

"You're not going to believe this," said Gail. "But I did too."

We stared at each other in total amazement.

"You go first, Mom."

"It was wonderful, and I truly believe she came to tell me she was all right, and for me not to worry about her." I related the details as the three kids hung on every word.

"Mine was similar," said Helen. "Megan was sitting on the couch in the living room, you know not sitting, but sprawled the way she usually did. She was dressed in that funny pumpkin outfit you made for her one Halloween, Mom, and I asked her what it was like to be dead. She said, 'It's OK. Not bad.'"

Gail went next. "I was standing in the passageway and could see Megan on the verandah. She was smaller, like only twelve years old or so, but her face was older, just as she was a week ago. She was dancing with Dad; she had her feet on top of his and was surrounded by a whole bunch of little boys I didn't recognize. She looked towards me, smiled, and we waved to each other, and then it was me dancing with Dad, and Megan was gone."

We were all quiet until I broke the silence.

"I can't believe it. Megan came to all of us last night. What a girl. I wonder if she visited Dad too." We were waiting on Giles to return from his apartment where he'd gone to change his clothes.

And probably call Paula—Stop that!

Mandy was sitting in the front foyer of the funeral home and rose to greet us. She hugged me warmly and said Scott expected us.

Good, she can talk to Eric while we're gone.

Now that the time had come to say our final farewell to Megan, I thought it strange I should feel so calm. Was it because she had come to me last night and prepared me for this moment?

I love you, Megan. Dearest heart, you have given me the strength I need.

Years earlier when my father had suddenly died, I made a compassionate trip back to England for his funeral; I had wanted to see him one last time. My two brothers accompanied me, but I was led into the viewing parlor on my own. I expected to be shown into another room or at least walk across the space to see him in his coffin. The room was very stark, devoid of any furniture or trappings and I remembered how shocked I'd been to see my father laid out on a table only three feet from the door. I vowed then if any of my relatives died, I would be the one to uncover their face; I wanted to lead myself to the fearful truth.

Scott took my arm and led Giles and me to a door off the main foyer. We decided to go in by ourselves first and then come back for Helen and Gail.

And there she was—*oh my God, Giles hold my hand, I am losing my nerve*. But Scott had respected my wishes; Megan's face was covered with a clean white sheet. I stood by the door and looked around the room: it was subtlety decorated in pale blue including the plush carpet. Soft music was playing and various vases of fresh flowers were strategically placed. I was impressed at how "nice" it was. Slowly we advanced.

For the next fifteen minutes I privately, silently, said my goodbyes to my beautiful, darling daughter. I caressed her hands, stroked her hair, spoke not a word and didn't shed a tear.

I felt Giles's hand on my elbow. "Shall we get the girls?"
I nodded.

My mind was now totally blank. I could neither see nor hear. It was as a cripple, a boneless bundle; I was heaped into the front seat of the car for the journey home up the interstate. What did I call it, the inferior vena cava? How many years ago was I full of jest traveling this same road to begin my first day in heart surgery? Such promise, so much excitement, in spite of the slight melancholic mood mourning the loss of my mother.

Mum, I beg you, take care of your granddaughter. Show her the path of eternal love. It must have been fate that you both should die on the same day, at the same time of the day, exactly ten years apart.

I tried to project myself five years hence, but it was impossible. With a heart so mangled and torn I couldn't foresee the next five hours, indeed I would be fortunate to survive the next five minutes. Fortunate? No. It would be fortunate if I died in the next instant.

Leaving the interstate, we approached an intersection where I spotted a green Toyota Corolla in front of us. Giles had seen it too, and we exchanged a look. We knew this make of car would always be associated with Megan. I glanced away, and tried to stop the flowing tears by biting the knuckle of my forefinger. I knew if I really let go now, I might never stop. I would cry an ocean of tears that could change the geographical map forever.

I felt Giles' hand on mine, a silent gesture of condolence. Thanks. The kids in the back seat had also seen the car. Nobody spoke, but gentle hands caressed me. I felt warm touches on my shoulders, tender fingers through my hair, and a hand brushed my cheek. I tried to yield to the power of touch, the enormity of love through impassioned suggestion. But it was not enough. The simple gestures of sympathy incongruously made it worse. We were on the move again and mercifully the Toyota turned left.

"Mom! Do fleas have noses?"

A flashback from the past.

The question floored me. It was at this intersection on the opposite side of the road. Dark, six-thirty in the morning, driving Megan to school. She was twelve. How to answer such a profound inquiry? I laughed of course, but this was quintessential Megan, a mind so unique, and so off the wall. How did she come up with such stuff? I didn't want to 'laugh' at her. Instead, as seriously as I could summon, directed her to answer the question herself. Was this something she was learning about in science class?

Parts of the body? Insects?

I decided I would do a little teaching myself, and instructed her to look up all words associated with "nose" and we would compose a poem to honor the flea. To and from swim practices, at times hysterically laughing whilst stopped at traffic lights, the poem slowly took shape. Me driving, Helen frantically scribbling and crossing out, Gail yelling to open every window, and Megan, with her nonsensical malapropisms, we all finally came up with this family's effort.

Do fleas have noses? I asked my Mom,
I don't know she said, try asking one,
To my dog Molly, I pleaded that night,
Help me out of this awful plight.
Give me a flea whatever the cost is,
So I can examine the creature's proboscis,
With critter in hand, and more than a week,
I still didn't know whether it had a beak.
After a while in sheer desperation,
I asked the small thing for its own explanation.
With a look of disdain and a bit of a pout,
Why should he disclose the existence of snout?
What is it worth to you, to tell?
Whether I can or cannot smell.

Oh Megs, you'll never be gone.

Chapter Twelve

Arriving home, I realized I was mind, body, heart and soul exhausted. The dear Lord must have been looking out for me because the house was empty, the phone temporarily quiet. I hadn't the strength to listen to messages or make the infallible tea. I told Giles I needed a break from the endless stream of well-wishers. I told the others not to disturb me, retreated to my bedroom, and closed the door.

Bone weary, too tired to cry, too fatigued to feel, I lay on my bed for the longest while staring at a single spot on the ceiling. I stared and stared, not seeing the minute break in the plaster pattern, but images of Megan.

Four years old: filthy and wet in the little red Wellington boots she refused to take off, even in bed. No clothes, just the boots.

Two years: 'gate eat me. 'gate eat me. 'gate eat me. Non-stop throughout a family trip to the Okeefenokie Swamp full of alligators. By the end of the day, we were all singing 'gate eat me. And I wished one of them had!

Tempestuous fifteen: stamping feet, slamming doors, refusing to partake of a family photograph because she had "nothing to wear".

Six years: the pelican through the window. We were living in

Costa Rica and spent a lot of time at the beach. One afternoon Megan woke from a nap and came screaming through to me.

"Mommy, Mommy, there's a pelican in my room."

I took her back to her bedroom to see the tiniest of sparrows perched on the window-sill. Such a small being to terrify such a small being.

Seventeen: the two hundred and fifty dollar prom dress.

"Mom, it's perfect. I absolutely love it. I've got to have it. It fits, it's perfect, and it's totally me. I love it. There is no other choice. Mom, listen to me: I have a plan. Put it on your credit card, and I promise to pay you back. Honest Mom, I'll work extra shifts, anything. Pleeeeze Mom, pretty please. Mom, if you love me…"

I do, I do…

"Mom, would you like a cup of tea?"

I could just make out Helen's profile by the light filtering through the open door.

It was dark outside.

"Um. What time is it?" I stretched out my legs and rubbed my eyes.

"It's about seven. I'm glad you slept, but thought you might want to get up for a bit. Otherwise you won't sleep tonight."

I yawned. "Thanks. And I would like some tea if it's made. Where are the others?"

"We're all here, just sitting around, talking. One or two people have stopped by, but they've gone now, and there've been lots more flower deliveries."

"Oh boy. The response has been overwhelming hasn't it? Just give me a minute and I'll join you."

Helen left, and in the half darkened room, I lay still for just a moment, quietly breathing, grateful for the silence, and pacified by a gentle calm that anointed me as surely as any soothing balm.

I knew Megan was at peace. Soon her earthly shell would be cremated, and it didn't matter to me when this would take place. It made no difference now.

Ashes. Some thought had to go into what I wanted done with those, but not yet. I had a lifetime to decide.

The telephone was ringing as I walked into the sitting room. It was Eric's Mom in Ohio. I breathed a sigh of relief that Eric wouldn't expect me to talk to her at this time. I was adamant about not talking to anyone tonight. It was family only grieving time.

As I sank into an armchair, Gail crawled on all fours across the floor to plonk herself at my feet.

"Why didn't you let Eric see Megan today, Mom?" There was no recrimination in her voice, just a simple question.

"I don't know," I told her. "But I think it had to do with wanting Megan to belong to just us; probably a last pathetic attempt to keep her all to ourselves for ever. Selfish I suppose."

"Eric really loved her."

"I know, and maybe it was a form of protection for him that I wanted him to remember her as she had been and not broken as she was."

"How could you bear to touch her?" Gail's voice, just a whisper.

"Darling, she was of my flesh. I created every cell of her body. The bond of love never dies, and I needed that final caress. One day when you have children of your own, you'll understand, although God forbid, you have to go through anything like this."

I hated myself. My mother's ghost had invaded the room to haunt me.

Just you wait my girl—when you have children of your own—you'll understand one day—it's for your own good. . .

It was official, I was now my mother.

I looked around the room. Giles was talking to Helen. Eric was still on the phone with his mother, and Gail with her head on her arms across my legs was falling asleep. I stirred.

"It's been a terribly long day. Why don't you go to bed?"

Without a word, Gail roused herself, glided up to give me a hug and left.

"I think I'm going too," said Helen. She flopped onto the arm of my chair, nestled her head close to mine and whispered, "I love you Mom."

"I love you too."

That left Giles and me. We looked at each other as complete strangers. The void was far more than the three-foot separation. What was happening to us?

Who are you? I don't know. Did I ever? Oh yes I did and I do now.

I watched him squirm in his discomfort of not knowing what to do next. Gone was the compassion of the morning; the warmth he'd generated sustained me only for seconds. I knew he wished he could go back to his apartment. One little word from me saying it was all right, he would have bolted through the door. I took some wicked satisfaction in not yielding to his desires. Without a word or gesture, but with sheer will, I forced him to stay. He was Megan's father and my husband, he owed me that. I would make him tough it out with me.

What nonsense I was thinking. Let him go. If he doesn't want to be here, what use is he? He certainly doesn't meet my needs and I can't help him if he won't open up to me. I've no idea what he's thinking or how he feels and I can get more comfort from my cat. Despair was setting in fast. I covered my face with my hands and let my fingers rub the tension from my eyes.

Go away Mum, no more wrinkle stuff tonight.

I heard Giles leave his seat and tell me he too was going to bed.

"Fine," I said. "I think I'll just sit on the stoop for a bit. I'll try not to wake you."

I turned out lights, lit a candle, and went to my favorite rocking chair on the porch. It was lovely; cool, quiet, except for the habitual frog coax, or occasional whippoorwill call. I was alone. No one needed me. The dogs sauntered through the gap they'd made in the screen netting long ago, and sat as close to me as possible. Thatcher raised his head and sneakily inched his cold, wet nose into my hand.

"I love you Thatcher."

I automatically stroked his head while staring out at the night sky. A three quarter moon, shedded bright light, and one by one I could see the flutter of stars filling their celestial spaces. My mind kept wandering back to Megan's first word—"star" It was fanciful I know, but I couldn't help seeing her as she was in my dream last night, floating, happy. This time, she was not enclosed in the space capsule, but 'swimming' between the heavenly bodies.

Twinkle, twinkle, little star—Oh Megs, I love you so. For what purpose has this happened?

I let out a deep sigh, slowly shook my head from side to side, and made no attempt to hold back the trickle of tears.

I don't know how long I sat there, but a chill in the air sent me shivering inside. Although Giles had his back to me, I could tell he was in a deep sleep. It was very comforting to slip into bed beside him and feel the warmth from his body.

Don't talk, don't think. Cast away sarcastic, derogatory thoughts, and definitely don't even consider sex. Wallow in nothingness.

A new day.

I couldn't remember what day it was. Was it the weekend

already? What did we have to do today? Should we go back to Daytona to see the girls in hospital? No I don't think so. I'll just call to see how they are.

The morning was like any other spring day in Florida. The house was quiet; nobody was up yet, except Giles who was drinking his tea in the rose garden. The odd thing was, I had nothing to do. No itinerary, no program, no demands. I'd come to the edge of the cliff.

That's impossible, I've always got something to do, or somewhere to go.

I poured my tea, and sat in the same chair on the stoop as I had last night.

Maybe this is my chance to stay here forever?

Less than thirty seconds went by before Giles spotted me and came to greet me.

"Good morning." He was cheerful. "I see you have some tea. Is there anything you'd like to discuss?"

What was this, a bloody board meeting? An inquisition? Stoppit!

You can't be mean so early in the day. Give him a chance.

"Well," I said. "What's the plan for the day? Is there anything we absolutely have to do?"

"No, not really," Giles replied. "Except maybe to meet with Pastor Kevin to go over the memorial service arrangements."

"And that involves talking with Scott. OK. I think I can manage this today. I'd like to get going with the plans. I have some definite ideas of what I don't want to happen."

"I'm sure you do," shot back Giles as he disappeared inside the house.

Was he being sarcastic? His tone unnerved me, but I decided to let it go and just sit and enjoy the morning glory.

I remained in my seat for the longest time until, of course, the inevitable ringing of the phone cut through the house waking others from sleep. Giles answered it, and shortly thereafter came to tell me

Ann was on her way over. I hoped it was a weekend day; I hated the thought of Ann losing another day's work.

I was a little bit hungry. *No!* A small sense of normalcy was creeping in, and why didn't I like that? It was only a few days since Megan had died; surely I wasn't supposed to eat just yet. Surely it was too soon for me to come back to life. Lack of nourishment was taking its toll; adrenalin was a poor long-term substitute for vitamins.

What's this? The sounds and smells of cooking drifted from the kitchen and to my disgust, I found myself salivating.

Don't move, don't say a word.

A few minutes later an arm reached over my shoulder from behind and there on a platter still hot and hissing was a fried egg sandwich.

"Eat," ordered the arm, "I'll make more tea."

I took the offered food and looked down to the slightly overdone lines on the toast, the little goblets of oil splattered on the plate, the soft buttercup yellow of yolk peeking between the two slices of bread and thought the most fabulous five-course meal could never compare to this. I ate slowly, not bothering to wipe the excess grease from my chin or fingers until I'd finished every last crumb. It was luscious, and I could have eaten six more.

"Thanks, Giles," I said to him as he sat beside me and began to eat his sandwich. "I needed that."

Ann suddenly appeared; we hadn't heard her arrive.

"Sorry to interrupt you," she said. "The back door was open and I could see you sitting out here."

"Don't ever be sorry," I said getting up from my chair. "Have you had breakfast?

Giles makes a mean egg sandwich." I smiled at Giles and patted his shoulder. "Come, I'll make you some coffee."

"That's all I need," said Ann. "How are you?" she continued, as we made our way to the kitchen. "How are you, really?"

My lovely friend: this was a heartfelt inquiry. How am I? For some unknown reason my brain reverted to an incident that had taken place years earlier at a local grocery store. The check out girl in the usual robotic fashion asked me "how ya doin' today?" "Bloody awful," I replied.   Without missing a beat between the dog food and soap powder, she said, "that's good".

I couldn't be that rude to Ann who was so full of genuine concern.

"I don't know Ann. I'm breathing, but it's like being starved of oxygen. I exist—gosh—I don't know. I keep thinking I'll eventually wake up from this nightmare."

"I only wish that could be true," Ann said. She held my hands in both of hers and looked me straight in the eyes. "I can't begin to understand your pain, but I do know you're the strongest person I've ever met, with unquestionable faith. God will see you through this."

I nodded. Many people in the last few days had told me the same thing in different ways.

I hated every one of them. Don't spout scripture or give me theories about God's plan or will, I don't want to hear it.

Maybe it was Ann's deep religious conviction giving credence to this simple sentence that I was fractionally comforted. I trusted Ann. God would have to wait.

Giles brought his empty plate in from the verandah and placed it in the sink. The three of us began discussing the arrangements for the memorial service barely two days hence. Format, numbers, music, food, invitations, no, not invitations but some kind of paper tribute.

"Paula can help us with that," said Giles. " She has her own studio, and I'm sure she can come up with a design depicting a swimmer. I'll call her."

I stiffened. *No ,no, no.* I didn't want Paula's help with anything, but I couldn't quickly think of a legitimate excuse of why she shouldn't be involved. I stood idly by while Giles dialed her number.

"Hey, it's me."

There was a pounding in my ears, my breathing quickened; my mouth set in a grim downward curve, and I wanted to throw up the wonderful egg sandwich.

"Come, Ann, let's take the dogs for a little walk."

She was out of her chair in a second, but not fast enough to catch me racing through the open garage. The dogs were scrambling to their feet at the sound of a rattling leash, thrilled at such an unexpected treat.

"What's wrong?" I heard Ann ask.

I slowed, panting now, "there's something going on between Giles and Paula."

Ann didn't speak, but let me rage.

"Does he think I'm a complete idiot? What the hell is he doing? At a time like this. Oh God give me strength. Je-**sus**, I can't take any more."

"Tell me," said Ann simply.

"Didn't you hear him," I screamed. "Hey, it's me. Not, 'Hello Paula, this is Giles.' Hey, it's me—like—"I mimicked the softened tone of a lover's familiar voice."—like that. Shit, he didn't even have to look up her number. What's happening Ann? All this bloody bullshit about us getting back together—sending Megan off to college—looking for a smaller property to buy—bastard—I hate him."

I leant against a tree, thoroughly drooped.

"You don't know for certain," Ann ventured.

"You're right I don't. But I do know. I feel it—in my guts—a wife's intuition if you like. You saw the way they were huddled together last night, or was it the other night, I don't know. I dismissed it because I was drunk and possibly seeing things, but today there was unmistakable intimacy. What the hell am I going to do?"

"Nothing right now. Listen to me; you've just been dealt the worst of all blows, more than any mother should ever have to cope with. You've got to put this to one side and get through the next couple of days. Helen and Gail need you."

I stood silently with my head bowed.

"Think of Megan and stay strong. If it means being ostrich like and ignoring this for the time being, then so be it. Deal with it later."

I looked at Ann. "I can't."

"Yes you can. For the sake of your own health, you've got to. You know I'll help in any way."

"My dear soul, what would I do without you."

We stood in the middle of the isolated dirt road, the dogs long abandoned to their own devices, and hugged long and hard. Ann was reluctant to let me go. It was as if she was trying to impart tenacity by touch.

We rounded the corner and saw several vehicles in the driveway. Good. Now I won't have to face Giles alone. I recognized one of the trucks, as CB's, a distinctive disheveled monster Ford, a bit like its owner.

Great. He's so full of his own importance and talks nineteen to the dozen; he'll take all the pressure off me.

Helen greeted me at the garage door with another hug. "Hello Ann," she said over my shoulder, and then releasing me, bent to stroke Thatcher. "Surprise," she went on, "both Gail and Eric are awake and up." She touched my cheek. " Mom, you look so tired, I hope you can bear with the mess inside."

Little did she know of my latest outburst. I was going to have to cope with anything and everything.

Here we go again, the same people. Did they camp out in the garden?
Computer Bastard was well established at the dining room table surrounded by all his things. I decided to be charitable.

"Hello, Jerry."

"Hey there. How are you? Look, come over here and I'll show you what I've done, and then if you could give me some more pictures, I'll scan them to make a power point slide show presentation at the service. See this photo here? That's my favorite. How old was Megan then? I've got an almost identical one of my daughter, she was five. I can attach music and any sort of graphic you want. I think it'll be great…"

"OK. Jerry." I cut him off. He was so bloody enthusiastic and even more cheerful. "I'll see what I can do." I wandered off to find Gail, but was intercepted by Giles. He put his arm around me, (guilty conscience?) and I hoped he didn't feel the tension in my body. I couldn't look at him.

"It's all set," he said. "Paula's coming over this afternoon with some samples for you to look at, and we can get them printed tomorrow."

"Whatever."

"What's the matter?"

"Sorry, Giles," now having to think up a quick lie, and disguise my body language. "I'm tired. Do you think you could take over for a while? Call Pastor Kevin. Tell him I want a very simple service, short introductory prayers, the slide show and then the chance for anyone who would like to get up and talk about Megan. Keep in touch with Scott at the funeral home. I'll talk to people on the phone if they need me, but I don't feel like doing much of anything today."

I couldn't possibly let him know how depressed I felt. Retreat and let the charade continue.

I sought out Gail, Helen and Eric and found them talking to each other apart from everyone else. Gail put her arms around me and whispered "I love you" in my ear.

"Mom, I hate to bring this up with everything else going on, but I've got nothing to wear for tomorrow evening's ceremony."

"No problem, Gail," I said. "I'll give you some money and you can go off to the mall. I want you to pick up a couple of CDs anyway. Music that Megan liked, and some of the stuff that was heard at swim meets. You'll know what to buy better than I, and I want to play some of those at the service."

"We'll all go," chimed in Eric. I think he was especially glad of the opportunity to leave the house and do something useful.

They left, and I went out to the verandah, content to be on my own and just sit. Minutes moved and I drifted in and out of reality.

I saw Megan eating olives from a jar against the wide-open refrigerator door. I strapped sprained ankles, bathed scraped knees and nursed that fractured collarbone. The last injury only two years ago. A lifetime of diapers. Then the laughter—the sheer delight of Christmas mornings—Megan's impatience, impossible to wait until after breakfast to unwrap presents.

The frustrations of English grammar and the arithmetic celebrations. Glory hallelujah, an 'A', in an otherwise average world.

Persistent to a fault—"why not?" "why can't I have?" Go to your room Megan and don't come out until you can behave in a civilized manner.

What I wouldn't give to tell her that just one more time, "Go to your room."

Oh the stretch of a teenager and the strains of the mother-daughter relationship.

Drifting again, a Chinese face appeared, a woman, young and pretty. Did Giles look at her with longing? What about that secretary, the floosie, and married with children to boot, who openly admitted to wanting an affair with Giles. Perhaps they did have. And who knew what he got up to on his business trips to Latin America?

Stop!

My grief was overwhelming and confused.   Megan? *Of course.* Giles? *Later- much later.*

There was a commotion going on behind me, and a toffee-soft voice from the past brought me back to earth. Rick! Was it really Rick Clapton from Costa Rica standing there with an enormous ceramic bowl full of every green fern imaginable?

"I came as soon as I heard," he said. "We're all devastated back home. I couldn't believe it. Not our Megan. Mary and the girls send their deepest sympathy."

He and his wife had three daughters more or less the same age as ours, and they all had gone to school together. Before I could say anything, Gail came bounding onto the verandah, followed closely by Helen, with Eric bringing up the rear. Everyone began talking at once, so I left my chair and briefly explained to Eric who this person was.

"We met Rick and Mary at a school PTA meeting years ago in Costa Rica." I told Eric. "As families, we spent a lot of time together, but I only tolerated Mary." I kept my voice low so Rick wouldn't hear. " But Rick, was friendly, gregarious, as much devoted to our children, as he was his own. We haven't seen too much of them since moving here."

However, it didn't surprise me to see him turn up now.

"Hello Rick." Here was someone who knew Megan as a little girl, pigtails and all; the acute implications brought new tears. "How good of you to come."

He gathered me in his arms. "I can't believe it. I can't believe it. I'm so sorry."

Giles was there now, and letting me go with one arm, Rick shook his hand.

"It's not fair," said Rick. "Megan was such a lovely girl—what a bright future. Helen, Gail—I'm so sorry. My girls talk about you often and will never forget the wonderful times we shared."

The noise level from inside the house had increased. I glanced over to the kitchen to see more people arriving.

When is this ever going to end?

Paula had arrived, and horror upon horrors she looked as though she was coming over to embrace me. I stood benumbed as ice, not giving her an inch. Giles quickly intervened, and put his arm around me. In the back of my mind I thought he must have spoken to her to tone things down, pay me more attention. I still felt out of the loop, and she still infuriated me.

"I've brought a copy of the stencil graphic for you to look at," Paula said. "If you don't like it I can do another."

"I'm sure it will be fine." I said curtly, and glancing down saw that it was indeed fine. *Dammit.* With a few effectively well-placed lines, Paula had depicted the bent elbow of the upward stroke, and head down of a free-style swimmer in water. It was perfect as a frontispiece for the memorial pamphlet.

"That's great," said Giles. "Thanks a lot for doing this."

"You're welcome. I'm glad I was able to help."

"Can I get you a beer?" asked Giles as he moved away from me and steered Paula towards the kitchen.

It's all legitimate now isn't it. Licensed to be together. Go on, provoke me some more, why don't you?

I stayed on the verandah and talked to Rick. Without a hint of intimacy, it was as though he were mine, a reminder of the past and my only comfort beside Ann and the girls. The rest of them belonged to Giles.

I was set at ease in Rick's company; his soothing words a great relief to the horror of the past few days. We reminisced about times in Costa Rica; he even made me laugh once or twice.

"Do you remember when Megan bit Steve Randall's bottom?"

I gulped and choked on my beer. "Oh my God, I thought I would die of embarrassment. What was she? Five? I don't know what got into her, but she was mad at him and his wife for something and his bottom was the nearest thing to her teeth."

We downed a couple more beers together before he looked at his watch.

"I'll be here tomorrow for the service. What time will it be?"

"Six o'clock," I told him. "Thanks for coming, Rick. It means so much to me, and thanks for cheering me up."

He took my hands in his, stood there slowly shaking his head from side to side.

"Words fail me," he said. " I don't know what—"

I cut him off. "It's OK. Rick." Gently now, "I'll see you tomorrow."

As he left the porch, Helen handed me the phone.

"It's Deni from Georgia," she said.

Deni was Megan's first swim coach, the most avid enthusiast of the sport, who not only gave invaluable advice but also became a very good friend. We car-pooled to swim practices and drove to meets all over Georgia together; my three girls and her two, we had the best and worst of times. Triumphs and disasters within a hundredth of a second.

"Deni."

"Oh my dear friend, I'm so so sorry. I can't believe it—what happened?"

"We don't know for sure, but Heather, the other girl who died and was driving—we think she fell asleep."

"Oh no. I didn't realize two had died. How awful. Oh my God—what can I do?

When's the funeral? I must be there."

"It's tomorrow Deni. Look, I know it's a long way to come, but I'd love to see you. I'm sure Helen and Gail would too. Why don't you come to the house and we can talk. The service isn't until six."

"That's a good idea. Just know you'll be in my thoughts until then. Take care, I'll see you tomorrow."

"'Bye."

I was alone on the darkened stoop, and continued to sit for a few more minutes, fancying the roar of the crowd, the smell of a chlorinated pool, piles of wet towels, cheers, jeers, desolation tears and victory waves.

All gone now.

Ann gingerly poked her head around the corner.

"How you doing?"

"OK. I suppose."

"I'm off home, but let me tell you, Jim called me from the restaurant and told me to tell you that all the catering is taken care of for tomorrow night. Prime rib no less."

"That's great Ann, and so generous. I hadn't given food a thought, there's so much here anyway."

"Yeah, well he can afford it. Don't forget Megan worked there, and you are a top-notch employee."

"That's nice, thanks. Ann, I'll see you tomorrow. And once again many, many thanks for everything."

"Good night, Ann." Helen's voice as they passed each other in the doorway.

"Is Deni coming?" Helen asked, undisguised excitement in her voice.

"It seems like it," I said. "Helen, I can't take any more calls tonight. Not one. I'm going to knock myself out with a sleeping pill and go to bed." I gave her the phone while squeezing her arm, a gesture I hoped would reassure her I was all right.

"I love you, Mom."

"I love you too. 'Night."

Chapter Thirteen

Nothing until morning.

Even though the sleep was chemically induced, it was much needed, and I woke refreshed. Giles was still beside me and I nudged closer. I needed him. I needed him. God knows I needed him. Seven o'clock in the morning had always been a good time for us. I dreaded the day to come.

Giles must have felt the sheets tighten because he was instantly awake. For a few amazing minutes we were the happily married couple of old. He put his arm around me and kissed me. I snuggled tight, basking in tenderness. I positively purred. Would that time stood still, but no.

"Do you think Megan is in Heaven?" I asked him.

"I really don't know," he replied, immediately releasing me and getting out of bed.

Bugger! Why did I do that? Why couldn't I relax for a moment and let Giles give me what he could, without the constant demand for more. That was a damn fool question at the best of times, let alone first thing in the morning, and today. You idiot, you've just allowed him to put up his emotional guard again, and God knows if you'll get him back at the time you need him most. The Memorial Service. Bugger!

"I've got to go into the office today for a short while," Giles said from the bathroom. "But if you need me, call, I shouldn't be long."

There. He was back on solid familiar ground.

"Good morning Roger," I said to my orange and white cat who had jumped onto the bed, at once filling the void my husband had left.

I couldn't be bothered to get up, and lay thinking how I hated crying and how much more of it I would be doing today. I was calm now, and dry-eyed, but I'd better start getting into shape for the challenging, heart-expanding endurance test tonight. Steel yourself; step back a pace; take a deep breath; control your tongue; practice your yoga. Ay! The very thought of it all put me in a dither.

"Mom, what would you like for breakfast?" Gail. What a pleasant surprise.

"A Bloody Mary please."

"Right on, Mom, I'll make two."

I knew she made the best Bloody Mary ever. I might even have another.

Rouse yourself.

But I couldn't.

Gail and I spent the next hour talking, she, lopped over the end of the bed while I made myself comfortable at the head.

We're united in misery, yet so content with each other.

"You remember the swim meet in Jacksonville last month Mom?" she paused, and then went on, almost inaudibly. "That was the last time I saw Megan."

The meet had been at the university pool. Gail and her boyfriend Keith had come to cheer Megan on.

"Yes, that was Megan's final swim. She was desperate to get a senior national cut in the backstroke, remember, and left it until the last race of the day. God, I was so nervous and I know she was. I also wondered how I would have coped with her if she didn't get it."

"No kidding. But, was she ever pleased with herself afterwards.

I can see her now, leaping out of the pool and rushing to give you a big hug. She didn't care that she was still sopping wet."

"Neither did I," I said.

Oh no, not more tears, but I felt myself welling up at the memory.

"Sorry, Mom, I didn't mean to make you cry. Here, I'll fix another drink."

"No, Gail. Too much alcohol, especially hard liquor, is not good, it makes me worse. I'll have a beer later on to steady my nerves. I'm on home ground with that. Where is Keith by the way?"

Gail gave out a disgusted snort. "Another emotional desert—makes me sick. He says he'll be here tonight, but I kind of doubt it. Says he can't cope—I don't care one way or another."

She obviously did, because she hastily left the room.

Sorry Gail, I can't help you with this one.

What was I going to wear tonight? Not black, maybe something flowered, pastel? How many people were coming back to the house afterwards? Did they have to be invited? Were there enough chairs? Who was taking care of all this? I must remember to feed the dogs before I leave.

Helen and Eric were up now, gone off to buy more CDs. "Reach" by Gloria Estefan, anything by Celine Dion (Megan loved her) and one more, a surprise requested by me.

Scott called from the funeral home telling me he would bring the service sheets to the house for us to fold. He would take the guest registers to the church. Everything was in order.

Giles called to tell me the venue had changed from the annex to the main church. Pastor Kevin had had quite a number of inquiries already this early in the day, and many flower deliveries, surmising the annex wouldn't be big enough.

What, more than two hundred and fifty people?

Giles would be home for lunch.

CB called wanting the music selection for the service. I told him the change of place.

"I'll get there around five to set up—the power point slide show's going to be great—I've put in all your favorite pictures and some of mine—hope you don't mind—I can't wait for you to see . . ."

SHUTTUP

Siesta time after lunch. The house was quiet, devoid of people save for the family, and I was grateful for the time out.

Deni arrived from Georgia, mid afternoon, driving a new black BMW, a present to herself from her divorce settlement. We had a beer to celebrate. I'd never liked her husband, and could now tell her so. We sat on the floor stamping the sheets of paper with Paula's stencil and then folding them in four. I wanted to tell Deni all about Paula, but decorum for time and place got the better of me. Anyway the kids and Giles were milling about and I didn't want to discuss her with them in earshot. Over and over we talked. Again, she reminded me of incidents I'd long forgotten about Megan.

"Remember when we were in that hotel in Augusta, and Megan overturned the table in a fit of temper because she'd just lost at cards? Maybe we shouldn't have laughed, but—just to see those cards fluttering all over the room. . ."

I chuckled. "Perhaps not. She was so competitive in everything she did. She hated to lose."

"I think what impressed me most," Deni said, "was her curiosity—her keen observations. She didn't miss a thing did she?"

"Not a thing."

I called Ann.

"Can you help me out this afternoon please, Ann?"

"Of course, name it."

"I'm going to the church early, and wondered if you could be there with me?"

"Sure."

"I would like you to be a sort of bodyguard. I don't want to speak to anyone before the service begins, especially people like chief mourner Nancy."

"Yeah, I remember her. Sure thing. Whatever you'd like me to do. Hey, you are still joking about the chief mourner thing aren't you?"

"Yes, of course I am. It's just that if I start talking to people, I know I'll cry and I want to stay strong, at least until after my speech. And I don't want to walk in to a crowded church and have people stare at me"

"I understand. I'll be there."

Immediately the phone rang again, but Giles said he would answer it.

"It's Channel 2 Television. They want to know if they can be at the ceremony to televise for the late news. What shall I tell them?"

"Tell them—hell I don't know—tell them—what do you think? Yes, they can come, but they have to stay outside the church."

Good grief, this was getting out of hand.

The doorbell rang. Thinking it would be yet another delivery of flowers, I answered, and immediately wished I hadn't. There stood Barbara Bentley, Melissa's Mom. (Melissa was the butterfly leg of Megan's relay team, and a truly lovely girl)

"Where's Megan?" Barbara asked and made to push past me to enter the house.

"Where's Megan?" I repeated and stood my ground. "Where's—well, she's certainly not here!"

"Well where is she?"

Good question. One I didn't answer—not to this woman on my doorstep.

"Barbara, thank you for coming, and I'm sure I'll see you later at the service, but I really can't cope with visitors this afternoon. I know you'll understand. I need to rest up now."

"Oh- yes- oh- all right—um—right, well—okay then. See you at six right? I'll pray for you, and may God rest Megan's soul."

"Yes, Barbara, and thanks again for coming."

"What was THAT all about?" asked Helen, who had just returned from her shopping trip.

"That was Melissa's Mom, a closet religious crank, often seen at swim meets with hands clasped, eyes shut and lips moving, praying her daughter would win the race."

"Talks a lot?" chimed in Gail. "Yeah, I've seen her and avoided her. A real Holy Roller."

"She means well," I said. "But did she really think I had Megan stretched out on the dining room table?" We all stared, incredulous of speech.

"Shame though, she probably thought she'd be done out of a good viewing." I said at last.

Four o'clock.

"Do you want tea or another beer?" asked Giles of Deni and me.

"Another beer please," we both said in unison, looked at each other, and laughed.

"They are slipping down very well," I said. "And are a marvelous tonic for nerves."

"Take it easy." Giles, cautious as ever, especially with alcohol.

Five-fifteen pm. Ann was waiting for us in the church parking lot. "You look nice," she said as she fell in step to one side of me.

"You can do this. You'll be just fine. God will give you the strength you need." She put her arm around me in a tight hold.

I looked at her and smiled.

As we entered the foyer, Scott greeted us. I could hear CB's voice above anyone else and quickly dispatched Giles to give him the music CDs. He was the last person I wanted to see.

The huge auditorium was empty except for a few church personnel. A photograph of Megan was highlighted on an enormous screen above the stage area at the front. Megan at eighteen. A sophisticated non-smiling Megan, beautifully made-up with her shining, brilliant hair cascading around her face. For the photograph she had rested her chin on her arms on a glass table. As she gazed out to the large sanctuary, her big brown eyes seemed to follow you wherever you went. I had a similar photo of my mother at the same age and although I had seen undeniable family likenesses before, I was staggered at how much like my mother Megan was. I lifted my head in silent prayer.

She's with you now, Mum, but please take care of me tonight.

It was early, but I sensed people arriving as Ann and I made our way down to the front seats. Sure enough, I glimpsed Nancy lurking down the side aisle. I turned, and gave her what I hoped would be a small wave of dismissal. Ann must have followed up because Nancy made no move towards us.

Giles joined me and we had a brief discussion with Pastor Kevin on the format of the service. I sat down with Helen and Eric beside me, and Ann immediately behind us.

Gail was jittery and couldn't stay still.

"Sit down, Gail." I ordered.

"Mom, I'll be back in a minute. I want to talk to Mandy."

"I'd rather you just sit."

"Mom, don't tell me what to do. There's nothing wrong with me talking to my friends."

I was disappointed that Gail should think this was a social affair, but had no power to stop her.

The church was filling fast, judging by the increased murmur of voices. Giles came to sit beside me.

"Are you all right?"

"I'm doing my best," I told him.

Laura had joined Ann behind me. I half turned and smiled a greeting to her. I felt Ann's hands on my shoulders, protecting me better than any British bulldog. My focus was straight ahead.

Breathe. You can do this—breathe—one, two, three. Deep breath in—out through your mouth. That's right, calm yourself.

I stared at the huge stage, an area that housed a choir on Sundays and theatrical performances throughout the year. I wondered how many yards of cloth it had taken to make the plush red velvet curtains. And how heavy was the wooden cross suspended from the rafters? I was glad the cross was bare. Simple. There was something about seeing Jesus being nailed to wood that unnerved me, and I needed all my nerves to be intact now. Look at all those flowers, equally as many as at home.

OH NO! In my peripheral vision I caught sight of Paula tripping down the center aisle and Giles got up to greet her. *Please don't*—but he did. With hands on her shoulders, Giles kissed her on both cheeks, European style. I'd never seen him do that before. *Another special thing between them?* Ann's hands tightened on my body. Keeping my head still, I reached up with one of my own hands to give her a reassuring pat.

My thoughts were interrupted by the lights dimming and a spotlight trained on Pastor Kevin.

"Welcome to Northland church," he began. "Let me explain what's going to happen here today. Megan's parents have asked that this not be a formal funeral service for their daughter. This is going to be a little more casual, giving us all a chance to think about the person we've known and loved, and an opportunity to say goodbye. Megan's parents have also requested that this be a time of joy, a time of celebration. How can this be, you ask. This sounds like a contrast; how can a time of death, and sorrow and sadness exist with a happy occasion? Well, the reason is twofold. One, that was the person Megan was, exuding joy and passion in the life she led. She also made a very clear profession of faith in the Lord Jesus Christ. To give her life to Him was a decision she made in her early teenage years, giving us an assurance of where she is now."

Here Pastor Kevin read from the Bible.

" 'I am the resurrection and the life. Whoever believes in me shall have eternal life.' We must be happy knowing Megan has eternity to celebrate with the Lord.

Secondly, Megan influenced many people in her life. Actually, this is what we're here for tonight, to remember what she did or how she impacted you. We will begin with a prayer, and then the family will come up on stage to say a few words. After that, anyone may join them in fellowship with a prayer or a story, a remembrance, anything you wish to say about Megan. Now let us bow our heads."

I did as I was told, and fiddled with my wedding ring. Eternal love.

"—this was a good day for Megan, but a terrible day for us," I heard Kevin say. Megan's squashed face appeared before me, wet and slimy, eyes screwed tightly shut, the instant she was born, before her first breath, before her first scream.

My own eyes stung with unfallen tears, "—Heavenly Father in your mercy... " Giles's voice, "Look, she's the image of Helen when she was born." "—hear our prayer..."

I can't do this. I can't get up there in front of all these people and talk about Megan.

I felt Giles's hand underneath my elbow, propelling me upwards out of my seat.

"Are you ready?"

"I think I'm going to be sick."

But, there was no backing out now. With Helen and Gail like sentries on either side, I meekly followed my husband up to the stage and the podium.

Giles spoke first. A steady, measured voice, an unruffled countenance.

"Thank you all for coming. . ."

Then something very strange happened. An incredible calm coursed over me. From a point on top of my scalp, I had this feeling like warm treacle trickling over my head, down my back and spreading to my arms and legs. I lifted my head, straightened my spine, and took a deep breath in. Was this God giving me the strength I needed? I clasped my hands loosely at my waist and looked out over the darkened auditorium to see a small bubble of dim yellow light hovering towards the back wall. What was that? Not a flashlight, nor yet anything electric. Maybe a reflection from the projection room above, but I could see the steady streams of bright light forming the spotlight. No matter, I concentrated on the sun-like glow, and heard Giles telling the listeners how Megan had been a keen lover of wildlife.

"...I would take her out at night to search for owls," he went on. "One night we came upon a family of red foxes, which is pretty rare and very exciting, especially in an urban area. I could hardly contain Megan from breaking cover to try and stroke them. Awesome, she kept whispering over and over again. Awesome"

Giles looked at me and we both smiled. I nodded my confirmation of the recounted story.

Giles continued," And then she would become fiercely defensive when a new crop of houses sprang up on land we'd crawled over. What's going to happen to all the animals, she would say. Where can they go? Nobody seems to care about them—I'd like to read a letter from Ohio—we must not forget another girl died in the accident— some of you may know, that of all the college scholarships Megan received, she'd accepted the one to Clemson—happy—no flowers please—donations to. . ."

My concentration was waning again. I thought about the owls Megan had collected over the years. The little crystal one, the one she had cross-stitched in the first grade, the large life-like ceramic one were among her favorites. She loved owls—portenders of death in some superstitious circles. That's bizarre.

" —and now I'd like to present Megan's mother."

That's me.

"And your wife."

"And my wife. Sorry"

That's for you Paula.

Everything I had proposed to say vanished when I stepped up to the podium and tightly gripped the sides. Even in the dim light I could make out an auditorium half full.

Jesus. That would mean there were approximately twelve hundred people out there waiting for me to speak. Enough to make the old knees shake some more.

I looked up to Megan's photograph immediately above me and slowly the words began to flow.

"I will begin by saying that I am honored to be standing here to witness this incredible tribute from you all for my daughter."

I paused. Tears were threatening to choke me so I swallowed hard. *Breathe.* I had to go on. *Megs?*

Giles came to stand beside me and put a reassuring arm around my shoulder.

Thanks, I needed that.

I brushed a single tear from my cheek.

"To meet Megan was to know Megan," I continued. "She made an instant and lasting impression, either good or bad. Her gregarious nature and free spirit meant she knew no strangers. The same effect was on me the minute she was born—step back world, Megan has arrived. There was nothing wishy washy about her. She was passionate about everything—some would even say bossy. I would say "bossy" when she forgot I was the mother and she the child." I heard a few consenting chuckles.

"Straight, oft times rude, always opinionated, brought out the brash side of her personality. On the other hand she was very caring and considerate, especially to animals and babies. I was often told she made a wonderful babysitter." Again I paused as the brief image of a small child "flying" high in Megan's arms flashed before me.

"I shall always remember her for being extremely funny with an uncanny knack of being able to diffuse a tense situation with a dry remark or a quirky look. Sometimes, often to the annoyance of others, Megan and I would look at each other and peel off into laughter, enjoying a silent joke only shared by the two of us. Funny stories within our family are too many to relate, so I'll tell you just one." I went on to share the pelican on the windowsill tale from Costa Rica.

I finished up by assuring Megan how much I loved her and would miss her. I also told her to behave herself. A silly, last desperate attempt to have the last word as a mother I suppose.

I pleaded with the angels to take care of her.

"For this is wisdom," I concluded. "To love, to live.

To accept what fate or the gods may give.

To ask no question, nor make no prayer.

But kiss the lips and caress the hair.

Speed passion's ebb as you greet its flow.
To have, to hold, and in time let go."

I stepped back to the loving huddle of my beloved daughters. Giles resumed his role as head of household and introduced first Helen and then Gail. I heard their words, noted the inflections and inclinations, but failed to register the content. I was spent. As each one stood before the podium, I was both amazed and terribly proud of their poise and composure. They were so eloquent, articulate—so incredible—so young, and they really loved their little sister. At that moment, how I loved them to bursting point.

Finally, Pastor Kevin asked us to resume our seats and invited anyone to come up and speak. Other than knowing Eric would speak first, we had no idea what to expect. Eric, bless his heart, made us laugh with "homework" stories of an eleventh grader, a manipulating Megan, when she lived with Helen in Ohio. He always regarded her as another sister, and having five older ones himself, was glad to have her as the youngest.

And then began a long stream of people. Some I knew well and some not at all. Forty and fifty-year olds from the running group, one spoke of her athleticism, another wrote a beautiful poem on how much he would miss her. Young girls too overcome with grief to speak at first, but eventually going on to give fine, endearing tributes. Others couldn't look at us: more still gazed out over our heads. And some went on just a little bit too long.

Shannon! Yes that's her name. Beautiful, beautiful child. Shannon told us she had a dream the previous night that Megan was dancing in her living room. Megan looked into Shannon's eyes and told her she was still alive. Shannon woke up the next morning to realize it was true. Megan was still alive—alive in our hearts and our thoughts. I love you Megan.

…you don't know me, but I was in Megan's Bible class--

…I met Megan in sixth grade--

…we became friends standing outside the classroom door on detention together—

…I'm the lady who organized swim meets at the rival High School.

Oh so that's what you look like.

Then there was Steven. Steven—preppie, in checked sports jacket and khaki twills. Steven with simply enormous ears. I instantly understood why Megan had never brought him home. But he was a delightful soul who told us he'd known Megan for two years, although he was student at another high school. *He's secretly in love with her.* . He had nothing prepared, no notes, but impressively I knew he spoke from the heart. He respected Megan. He told us she was a great friend to him. They praised the Lord together, and we should be very proud of her faith.

The line seemed endless. The last of the honorariums included Megan's swim coach who reiterated the glorious triumphs of the previous year's state swim meet, and how proud he was to have her on his team. Several teachers were gentle and kind with their remarks. Megan was no brilliant scholar, but almost to a man (or woman) they made it clear to the listeners how unique she was, and how she would never be forgotten.

It was lovely.

Eventually the slide show began with background music, "Reach" by Gloria Estefan and "We are the Champions" by Queen. CB had done a magnificent job with the photographs, placing them in no particular order, but with cute captions or comments. I heard cheers at the state swim trophy celebrations. I heard lots of laughter, and then towards the end nothing but sniffles and sobs. Goodbye Megan.

It was over.

Lights came up; Pastor Kevin again thanked everyone for coming.

"We've heard tonight what a joy Megan was," he said. "Passionate and caring, and how much she gave to so many. Remember the words from her obituary, how she kept her eyes on the prize—an Olympic medal. Christ took hold of her for His purpose even greater than a medal, the prize of eternal life with Him. Lord Jesus we thank you and praise you. We thank you for the person Megan was. In the future there will be many more tears, bring us back dear Lord to the hope and security of faith in You."

Pastor Kevin looked out to us all with arms outspread and a huge smile on his face.

"Go forth in peace," he beamed." And I encourage you to take one particular gift home—something that Megan has given you that changed your life, how her marvelous spirit has enlightened or charged you. Now, I ask that you let the family out first. Goodnight."

A few seconds later as we began to file out, the earth-shattering sounds of The Village People blasted out "Y.M.C.A." filling the solemn space. I kept my head down, but could sense surprised smiles and looks of astonishment. It was my idea. Knowing everyone would be sad and tearful, I wanted to lift their spirits as they had done for me throughout the evening. I also knew most of them would picture Megan on a swim block dancing out the actions of the famous song.

"Y.M.C.A." was cranked out at every swim meet to get the competitors up and going, and Megan was notorious for leading the team.

As we left the auditorium, Ann told me she was quickly going home to pick up her husband Kenny. She'd see me back at the house.

"It was a great service, don't you think?"

"Fantastic," I whispered.

The foyer of the church soon overflowed with hundreds of well-wishers eager to pay their last respects. Our family became separated by the massive sweep of people. Helen and Gail were engulfed with their old school friends, and I could see Eric sticking close to Giles. Some faces I hadn't seen in years—swim kids all grown up, recognizable now only with their parents. Faces I knew were familiar, but couldn't quite put a name to. Grinning faces, teary ones, and some so grim, they made me cry. I smiled a lot too, in an effort to ease their pain. Such diversity of thought, sharing poignant moments in rapid succession with so many.

Gosh! There's my friend, Linda, from Miami, I didn't know she was coming. I hope to see her later, she knew Megan from two cells old.

More than several colleagues from the restaurant had shown up, and I idly wondered who was left to mind the store.

I found myself affected in a weird way. It had been a wonderful ceremony—uplifting—exhilarating—overwhelmingly supportive. Now, this could be a wedding reception, or a family reunion, there were so many people greeting me, and each other. The only person missing was Megan, and I knew how much she hated to miss a good party. Somehow though, I believed she wasn't actually missing a thing. So many of the high school kids left without acknowledgment; I couldn't blame them, teenage kids who had lost a dear friend had no idea what to say to parents.

Kathy from my school appeared by my side.

How many years ago was I in surgical tech school?

"Betty (our teacher) sends her sympathies and her apologies for not coming. She doesn't do funerals."

"My God, Kathy, did she actually say that?"

"Yes, she did. A few of our classmates didn't know whether to come or not, but I can tell you they're all pretty upset. Don't worry about them, if you need me, just call. I'll be in touch very soon."

"Don't you want to come back to the house for a while?"

"I'd like to, but I have to get up early. Stay strong. I'll call you."

"Thanks, Kathy. Thanks for coming, it means a lot to me." She was gone.

By the time I finished my brief conversation with Kathy, most of the throng had left. Gail told me she was going back to the house with her friends. Helen and Eric left in their rental car. So, that left Giles. Where was he? The remaining few stragglers were leaving and panic was quickly setting in. Where was Giles? There was someone, whom I barely knew, but knew him to be a running friend of Giles. I approached him.

"Have you seen Giles?"

"Oh, well—yeah, I think he left already."

Boom.

A fat smack to the side of the head, a body blow to the gut.

Mouth open, I stared at this comparative stranger.

"Did you see him go?"

"Yeah, sometime ago. He was with James, I think."

And so it was, that I staggered out to my car alone. I didn't know whether to cry, vomit or commit murder.

How could Giles leave me to drive home on my own after my daughter's funeral?

I was beyond feeling. It was unbelievable.

Rock of ages, cleft for me, let me hide..."

Chapter Fourteen

Five miles—stop signs, traffic lights, turn signals, people on sidewalks—I saw nothing. I remembered not one single thing. I turned the last corner to my home, and returned to reality and despair. Cars lined the street, driveway and grass, leaving me no room to park. Sure, the garage door was wide open and empty, but I couldn't get my car in there. Sod it; I parked sideways behind two cars, effectively blocking them in.

There must have been two hundred people overflowing my house. I'd never seen anything like it. I sought out Giles, who was outside with his running mates. He looked up from pouring beer.

"Hello, would you like one?"

Stay calm.

"Giles, why did you leave me there? I've just come from the church on my own." I kept my voice steady, but I was a nervous mess inside. Without wasting a drop, and in a tight, controlled, almost angry way Giles said," I told you I was going to check on the keg of beer with James."

If I were destined to have a heart attack, it would have been at that moment. I was struck dumb, too incredulous to speak. I stared at him, too unsteady on my feet to move, cocooned in such a state of shock I became a granite block of pain. What had I done to deserve this?

Keg of beer — getting my wife home from our daughter's funeral service. Keg of beer — being a kind, caring husband. Keg of beer — responsibility for...

"—I've never seen you more gracious than you were tonight."

I felt a hand on my arm, and turned to face my co-worker Peter from the restaurant.

"Thank you, Pete. Thank you. And thank you for arranging all this food, it's great."

And thank you for bringing me back to earth. I'll deal with Giles later. I have responsibility to guests other than runners.

Peter and I walked back onto the stoop together, where every well-intended sympathizer swallowed me up. The free flowing alcohol had loosened tongues; the noise level was on the rise. Gail saw me and came rushing over.

"Mom, you were awesome tonight. I love you so much. I'm so proud of you, and Megan would have been too. Come and say hello to my friends." She steered me to the other end of the stoop, where, as I got closer, I was impressed to see the young men stand. Perfunctory greetings to those I knew slightly, and big hugs for the girls and boys whom I knew through both Gail and Megan. Bigger hugs for Scott and Mandy.

"Scott, I can't thank you enough. What would I have done without you at the Funeral Home? The service tonight was beautiful — you did a fantastic job arranging it. Thank you."

"I'm glad I was here to help," replied Scott. " I think it went quite well, and I'll bring over the guest books tomorrow. I'm guesstimating there were over a thousand people there, judging by the signatures, although not everyone signed of course."

"Come anytime," I told him. "I'll be here for a couple of weeks. I'm not planning on going back to school in a hurry."

I greeted other guests: wove my way through awkward situations and extricated myself from strained attempts at conversation.

Hello, thank you for coming—how kind—yes, I promise to call if I need anything—sorry—wonderful service wasn't it—I don't know how long I'll be out—thank you—

"Sorry" is one sorry word and when repeated over and over again, becomes even sorrier.

I'm so tired.

Helen was a few steps from my side at all times, and Ann never took her eyes off me. I felt immersed in love and compassion, virtually shored up by benevolent tenderness. I avoided Giles straight out. I turned away from each of his cronies, especially Paula. Resentment? Oh yes. Resentment towards the ones who never knew Megan or me, and were here seemingly for the beer alone. Yet, in my fragile state, I could not afford to risk Giles's wrath by confronting him. I knew he would defend every last one of them, and I hadn't the energy or will to argue.

Not all from the running group were shallow and uncaring. I checked uncharitable thoughts as I watched Jane and Karen begin to tidy up. They had both loved Megan dearly, and were solidly upholding me.

"Thanks, girls," I told them. "Can I help?"

"No," said Jane firmly. "We don't want you to do a thing."

"You're so good to me, I really appreciate this. Don't get me wrong, but I wish everyone would leave. I'm just about done in."

"I'm sure you are," said Karen softly. "We'll do our best to herd our lot out of here as soon as possible." Just as she finished saying this, Giles came to me with phone in hand.

"It's Wendy and Vince from Atlanta, they want us to come up this next weekend."

"I don't know—it's too soon..."

"Talk to them, they're very concerned. We've got the money, if you want to go. It's up to you."

I took the phone from Giles and wandered off into the garden.

Everyone had gone except Jamie. He and Giles were outside finishing off the last of the beer. Gail, Helen and Eric had either gone out, or to bed, I didn't know, but the house was blessedly quiet. I picked up stray glasses and took them to the kitchen, and then went out to put my car away, but someone had already moved it.

Cigarette butts in the driveway, how disgusting.

I rounded the house with Thatcher by my side. He kept nuzzling my hand, begging for attention, so I bent down and nuzzled him back.

"I love you Thatcher. I love you, I love you, I love you." He barked his approval and ran off for additional petting from Giles.

James and Giles were laughing as I drew near. Were they drunk?

"I think we might go to Atlanta for the weekend," I said to Giles." Wendy was very persuasive—it could be the right thing to do. I'm going to bed now; we can talk about it in the morning. Goodnight James, and thanks for your help with the drinks, extra tables and all."

*I remembered **my** manners.*

"No problem," he said. I moved forward to give him a hug. He was another who had been devoted to Megan, but found it difficult to express in words.

I flopped into bed, exhausted—physically and spiritually spent. I actually wished Giles would go back to his apartment. Still on the emotional roller coaster as far as he was concerned, I couldn't decide whether I was up or down, right side or wrong side out. Did

I want to go to Atlanta with him? Yes? And No? Long ago I'd made a contract with myself not to make any major decision after the sun had set, so sleep was in order now.

Good night, my darling Megan.

Giles hadn't gone back to his apartment, but I hadn't known when he'd come to bed, either; I must have slept an exhausted sleep. As I woke, it took a few moments to realize what day it was. A back to normal day? A regular, clock-work precision, back in the groove day? An ordinary day for the rest of the world, maybe. Megan was gone; my world was so profoundly changed, that nothing, or no one, would ever be the same again.

Helen and Eric and Gail were leaving today. No doubt Giles would stay in the office until well after six. What was I going to do? Cry some, and then some more. Cry buckets. Cry, cry, cry.

I'm a crybaby; that's the only thing I know how to do really well.

Thank God I was going to be on my own. I hardly wanted to clean my teeth, get dressed or bother to eat, much less talk with anyone. *Only you, Megs.* I wanted to void the day. Wander and wonder. Reflect and recoup.

I said nothing about the previous night as Giles dressed for the day. What was the point? He had no idea what an arsehole he was, and there was nothing I could say now to make it right. My feelings for him were still very confused. How could my husband of nearly twenty-five years be so cruel?

Stop! Don't dwell on him; you'll wear yourself out.

"I'll be home for lunch, if that's all right with you?"

"—Um—wha'—sure—whatever."

"Are you O.K.?" Giles approached and made to embrace me. I turned away; I didn't want him touching me.

"I'm fine." Short, sullen, drained of feeling.

Go.

"Do you want to talk about going to Atlanta?"

"Later." I said. "I'll think it over."

Go!

Thankfully he did.

Helen and Eric had flights to different locations, but left together. Nothing much was said, it was a teary parting, this daughter and I knew the bond between us had strengthened.

"Call me." We had said to each other. We would.

Gail left shortly afterwards, and again it was oh so painful.

Don't go. Don't leave me on my own. Don't leave me with these demons. Don't—dear God—help me please—I can't face the future alone—

Gail had to go; she had classes to attend, and final exams looming. My moment of panic faded as I put on a show of stupendous strength, belying the ridiculously pathetic, pink pajama-clad shell, standing in the driveway waving a fond farewell.

Isn't this what you wanted? Now you are utterly, truly alone. Get on with it.

I looked around. Tire tracks had ruined the lawn and scuffed the flowerbeds. Remnants of the previous night's "party" were everywhere; there was even a small white car parked down the street, left by someone obviously too drunk to drive.

Cigarette butts are not biodegradable. I knew I'd have to pick them up sometime, but not now. Red lipstick stains would have to fade.

Soak in the sun; watch Roger stalking a squirrel in the neighbor's yard. Go get 'em Rog.

I haven't a clue how long I stood there, aimlessly staring. I couldn't have cared less who saw me. My "nothing" day had begun.

Or had it.

The shrill peal of the telephone interrupted my peace. I'd vowed to speak to no one today, until I heard Linda's voice on the answering machine. My dear friend. She was still talking when I reached the phone, and broke off the message.

"Hello Linda."

"Oh, hi—I didn't know if you'd be home, or if you would want to talk to anyone today. My mother and I are heading back to Miami, and as we missed you after the service last night, I wondered if we could pay you a visit before we left. That is if you feel up to it. I promise we won't stay long. How are you? Sorry, I shouldn't have asked you that. Sorry—stupid of me."

There's that word "sorry" again.

"I'm all right, Linda, thanks. Just tired and kind of numb, but yes, please come on over, I'd love to see you," I lied.

I did want to see Linda. No, I didn't. *Hell, the timing's not right.* I'm in mourning. I need the Victorian way, a black veil, darkened room, a sedative and silence. Wake me up for my funeral.

I meandered through the house with no clear direction of what I was doing. I made a fleeting mental note that the place was untidy and I had visitors coming.

Tut, tut. This won't do. Oh, to hell with it.

Years of habit forced me to pick up clutter inside the house, but I couldn't be bothered with the stoop. Leaving the French doors open, I sat down out there, staring into space, seeing only a great mass of grey. The tables were bare now, save for the soiled, once white, cloths borrowed from the restaurant. Extra chairs had been neatly stacked against the wire netting screen, for pick-up later, I presumed. I didn't know. As usual, the two dogs had found me and lay sprawled at my feet.

The telephone rang again, this time I ignored it completely. I heard a male voice, possibly Giles; yes it was, something about lunch. I had a strange metallic taste in my mouth—like chewing gum wrappers. I sat there and wondered how grief had affected my whole body. My heart was broken, my gut destroyed, and what little left of my brain, was mush. I'd chewed my fingernails, and neglected my skin. Did I clean my teeth this morning? I looked and felt like an old hag; how on earth was I going to recover from this?

When the ocean meets the sky you'll be sailing…

The doorbell rang, and thinking it would be Linda and her mother, I roused myself to answer it. It wasn't them but Kyndal, the breaststroke leg of Megan's relay team. Dressed simply in the uniform of summer, T-shirt, shorts and flip-flops, she looked so forlorn, a shadow of her normal boisterous, chatty self. She had tears in her eyes, and was biting her lower lip.

"I can't stay," she said. "And I probably shouldn't have come, and I'm sorry to disturb you, but I –" she sniffed and wiped away the tears with the back of her hand. "I just had to know if you were OK."

Tears began to flow down my own cheeks as I gathered this wonderful child into my arms.

"My dear girl," I mumbled. "This is the nicest, kindest thing you could ever have done—to check on me. Don't ever be sorry for coming, and you are welcome here any time."

We were both sobbing by now, and I stepped back inside the house for a tissue. Kyndal hesitated, and then followed.

"I miss Megan so much," she was choking on the words. "I don't know—how—I miss her so much."

"I know. I know."

Good grief, how Megan was blessed with so many wonderful friends, and why did I deserve such incredible consideration.

I held Kyndal's hands in mine, and looked into her eyes.

"I don't know how we're going to get through this either," I said.

"I can't begin to advise you how to cope. But I do know that the out-pouring of love shown to my family and to me has been utterly amazing. The only thing I can do is try to live for the moment. Don't wonder about the future without Megan—just remember her and the love she had for you."

Head bowed, Kyndal nodded her agreement.

"It was an awesome service last night wasn't it." She eventually said looking up. "And I'm sorry I broke down."

"Don't be sorry, you were marvelous," I told her. "Yes, it was the most incredible tribute—the most sincere—the most—the loveliest…" fresh tears from me now.

" Gosh Kyndal, I had no idea Megan was so well liked. Sometimes as a parent we get caught up in the daily disciplines, the tugs of power, the arguments of growing up, that we forget to enjoy our children as much as we should. Now it's too late."

It was a matter of fact statement. It was too late.

I wasn't actually looking for consolation at this precise time, feeling somewhat anesthetized from pain, but Kyndal tried her best.

"She loved you so much," she said. "She was always telling me how much she admired you, and wished she could be more like you."

"Thank you, you're such a sweet girl."

We embraced, and over Kyndal's shoulder I saw Linda's unmistakable silver Mercedes draw up to the curb.

"Please come to see me again, and when I get around to sorting out Megan's clothes, I'd like you to have some of her swim suits if you would like them."

"I'd be honored, thank you."

My two new visitors passed Kyndal in the driveway with a brief acknowledgement.

Deep breath in. Next.

The three of us sat on the stoop making small talk. It was an effort for me to make an effort, so I let them ramble on about Megan's early years. They certainly meant no harm; they were wonderful caring people whom we'd known for many years, but my heart wasn't in it. I zoned in and out hoping to interject the right response at the right time. Yes, yes I remember—she was so funny—how old was she then—sorry—unique—you're right—no, nothing thanks—sorry…

Sorry, sorry, sorry, sorry, sorry, sorry, sorry—my head buzzed like a violin bow grating across strings.

I was actually glad to see Giles walk across the grass. Was it lunchtime already? He was carrying a brown paper bag in one hand and a newspaper in the other. His face lit up when he saw Linda.

"How nice to see you." He kissed both Linda and her mother and added. "I've brought lunch, but there's more than enough food in the house if you'd like to stay."

"No, no, thank you, we must be going." *Thank you God."* We have a long drive ahead of us and I want to be back by dark." Linda looked at me and we embraced. "My dear, what more can I say. Trust in God, He will see you through this."

Well, He's done a hell of a job so far, hasn't He?

"Take care. Come and see us in Miami," added her Mom.

"I'll walk you out," said Giles.

I was left alone with mental images of a ten-year old Megan, dressed in a skimpy blue and white striped bikini, with a ruffle across the bust, hands on skinny hips, arguing some long forgotten point with Linda's attorney husband. I saw the smile on Hank's face as he goaded her deeper and deeper into tripping over her own words. Megan's face getting redder and her frustration with him more so; until finally with a flippant toss of her head she flounced off muttering he was impossible. I remember Linda chiding her husband for taunting a young kid.

"Nonsense," he had said. "Builds character."

How right you were Hank.

"Come and get lunch," Giles yelled from the kitchen.

"What's in the bag?" I startled Giles who had not seen me approach.

"I knew you wouldn't have eaten anything, so I stopped by that hole in the wall on 2nd Street and picked up your favorite Greek salad. Thought it would make a nice change from the stuff we have here."

I went to him.

"Put your arms around me, Giles. Thanks. That was very thoughtful of you."

We stood close together. I needed him despite his deplorable behavior the night before. I soaked in the familiarity.

Did he need me?

"Right, let's eat."

Don't ask. Don't get too close. That's enough now.

Over lunch the decision was made to go to Atlanta on Friday after work. Giles's secretary, Rosa, would book the airline tickets and Giles would call our friends, Wendy and Vince this afternoon.

All was quiet. The windows were open and a breeze floated the sheer curtains of my bedroom. I lay on my bed with Roger in his usual position at my side. From time to time he would open one eye, stretch, and casually lay a paw on my arm. Who was comforting whom? It could not have been coincidental. I'd never had another cat like him to be so intuitive to my needs. I reckon I had the better deal.

I wanted clarity, I tried to sort my thoughts—to put them in some sort of order, but every which way I turned it always came back to "how the hell am I supposed to cope with any of this?" There were no skills left and I'd run out of emotions—absolutely drained of feeling, the tank of tears bone dry, I even found it impossible to be angry with Giles or the world anymore. God was another matter. My nothing day was ticking away and I was nothing.

I must have dozed off because the awful alarm of the telephone forced my hand. It was Helen, delayed in Atlanta because of thunderstorms.

"Are you all right Mom?" she asked. "I hated leaving you this morning, and I want you to promise, that you'll call me day or night—anytime it doesn't matter, if you need to talk. Even if you don't want to talk, I'll be there for you. I love you Mom."

"Thanks, darling. And you do the same OK.? Listen, your Dad and I will be going to Atlanta for the weekend, and if the weather stays so bad this afternoon, call Wendy. I'm sure she wouldn't mind putting you up for the night. Don't fly in a storm."

My paranoia at losing another child had begun.

"Don't worry, I'll be fine. It's beginning to clear. Yep, they've just announced boarding. I love you Mom, I love you."

"I love you too. 'Bye."

Had I told Megan I loved her before she left for the beach? I didn't think so. I was still so cross with her for messing up the driveway with her scattered stuff, for not cleaning up after herself when she knew I was expecting possible house buyers. We'd come to a truce, and in her own indomitable, mocking way, Megan had made me laugh in the end. I could still see her grinning face poking out of the car window.

"Chill, Mommy."

But, I hadn't told her I loved her.

Chapter Fifteen

The telephone's renewed ring made me jump, and because I took so long deciding if I should respond or not, the answering machine came on.

"Hello, this is your realtor, Jennifer speaking. Just to let you know we still have parties interested in your property. Call me when you feel up to showing the house again, and we'll reinstate the sign. Take your time, there's no rush; everyone here knows how difficult this all must be for you. Take care. 'Bye."

There's another one getting back to normal. How long is normal grieving? Normal—normal—normal, a second word like "sorry" to add to my list. How odd though, that I should be thinking about the house when my realtor called. I'll speak to Jennifer tomorrow, or the next day or even the day after that.

Don't anyone ask me to make decisions yet.

A few minutes passed in silence before the phone rang yet again. Such a jarring sound to disturb my nothingness. But, it was Gail.

"Hello, Mom. I'm back. Thought you'd like to know."

Thank you, God.

"Yes, thank you darling, for calling. I'm sure you understand, I'm a wee bit nervous of the I 95 for the time being. Did you have a good trip?"

"Yeah. Not much traffic, until I hit Jacksonville. Everything's fine. Jimmy (her tabby cat) was pleased to see me, but I don't think Sarah (her roommate) was. I think she enjoyed being on her own. But, too bad, I'm here."

Strangely, I was finding it difficult to make conversation. Strangely because Gail and I usually prattled on for hours. "OK, Gail, take it easy, and don't work too hard."

"Mom, I'm here if you need me. I love you."

Two wonderful daughters.

"Me too. Oh, Gail, I nearly forgot to tell you, Dad and I are going to Atlanta for the weekend. Wendy was so insistent, and maybe it's the right thing to do. I don't know. There's a run scheduled for Saturday up there, and your Dad thought it might be nice to see other old friends from when we lived in Georgia."

"When are you going?"

"Friday after work."

"Good, Mom, like you say it might be the best thing for you to do right now—get you out of the house for a while. Who will look after the dogs?"

"Oh, thanks for reminding me, I must call Ann. I'm sure it won't be a problem for her. Well, Gail," I heard the beep of the call waiting signal. "I have another call, so I'll let you go, I'm sure you have lots to do, but thanks for everything, especially letting me know you're back home safely. I love you. Talk to you later."

"'Bye, Mom, I love you too."

I switched lines, and who should it be but Ann. *What was going on?*

"Hello."

"Ann, that's weird, I was just thinking about you."

"Is that right? I waited to call you until now hoping you'd be able to get some rest. How are you?"

"Distant, not quite here."

"That's understandable. Have Helen and Gail gone?"

"Yes, everyone left this morning, and I was hoping to be by myself for a bit, but that didn't happen." I gave Ann a brief synopsis of my day, including the decision to go to Georgia.

"Would you mind feeding the dogs please, Ann?"

"You don't have to ask, of course I will."

"Thanks. What would I do without you? It will only be for a couple of days, until Sunday night. Would you like to come for a beer after work?"

"Do you want me to? You don't want to be on your own for a while? Is Giles still staying with you?"

I understood Ann's reluctance. She didn't want to interfere in what ought to be a tender, evening between grieving parents.

"Yes, he's still here and probably will be until after the weekend. But I have a feeling he wants to work late tonight to catch up, but would worry that I'm on my own. At least, I hope he would worry. I don't know, Ann, after last night's debacle, I can't begin to know what's going on in his mind. I'll tell you about it later. I would really like to sit with you, quietly, just the two of us. It's over; everyone has gone. I haven't the first clue how I'm going to cope, and I'm scared."

"You know I'll help in any way I can."

"I know that, Ann, and thank you. But you're not me. I've got no choice but to feel all this, and, I don't mean to be rude, especially to you, but "I'm sorry" doesn't help one bit."

"Try not to get too far ahead. Take it one second at a time, and then one minute, and don't be too hard on yourself. Look, I will come for a short while after work. Do you need anything?"

"Are you kidding? I reckon I can live for three months on the food in this house, and there's nothing else that can't wait. But thank you."

"OK, see you later." I hung up the phone.

It was late afternoon, and pretty obvious I was not getting the solitary day I thought I wanted. This might be a good time to call Clemson University and speak to the head Swim Coach—let him know his top recruit would not be starting for him in August. I had to dig deep to remember his name—John? Joe? I'd have to look it up. Megan had had several college coaches very interested in her, but finally the Clemson coach won out with my child being his first pick. And she was going to be given a full scholarship. I remember how excited he'd been to discover she had a British passport. His goal was to train her not only for his university team, but also for the Olympics, where she could have swum either for Britain or her birthplace, Belize. Megan had been thrilled at the thought of going to Australia.

"Hell no," she had said in the past. "I don't want to go to Atlanta in '96, that's in America; I want to go overseas to Sydney in 2000."

I had thought about this for a while. Realistically, what were her chances? As her mother, of course I always thought she was better than she was. But I also knew her potential was beyond what she thought she had. For her junior year in Ohio, Megan had exceeded all expectations, even surprising herself. But this was all due to Coach Bob, who had recognized when to lead and when to follow. He had truly known Megan for all her strengths and weaknesses in and out of the pool. I felt this would have been similar with what'shisname at Clemson.

Joel! I knew it began with a 'J' Score a small victory for memory.

Before I could dial the number, the telephone was ringing again. This time it was my school friend Kathy. She would have been in class all day today. What do I do?

I let the answering machine pick it up.

OK. OK. I know she's concerned about me, and I probably should have

spoken to her, but I didn't want to. All right? I couldn't care less if I never
go back to school again.

Bugger! The bloody phone won't stop ringing now. Betty, my
surgical tech teacher.

She can wait too.

Jane, my brother Michael in England. (*It must be midnight over*
there.) Scott from the funeral home, some friend of Giles I'd never
met—*Hell, they can all go there.*

I drank a beer while listening, got myself thoroughly demoralized
and couldn't face calling the Clemson coach.

Giles can do it.

I wandered outside. My poor neglected roses. They badly
needed water.

Here, I hope you like salt water; let me cry over you.

But, I couldn't summon a single tear.

I sat on the little stone bench in the middle of my rose garden
and ran my palm over the defect on one corner. Daylight was
fading, but I could clearly see the scratch and missing cement. Years
ago on a Saturday morning in Home Depot, we'd bargained for a
50% discount for that minute nick. Where were you then Megan?
What were you doing at that precise moment? Touching the wall
of the pool at swim practice? Sleeping? Snoring? Chatting with a
girlfriend? Now, I wish I'd never let you out of my sight. If I'd known
this would happen, I would have glued you to my side.

But you did know something like this was going to happen. Remember
all those years ago how you knew one of your girls would not reach her
twenty-first birthday.

A shudder came over me, like Megan walking over my grave. I
rested my elbows on my knees, and closing my eyes massaged my
scalp with both hands. I'd been through too much to take in any
more. Some of the recollections were very painful and impossible

to dismiss. Others, though happier, made me sadder. I was sinking into the deep dark hole of depression spreading at my feet and was vaguely aware I was rocking from side to side. So tired, I wanted nothing more than to sit here, undisturbed, until a time I didn't have to think anymore.

"Is that too much to ask?"

A gentle touch on my shoulder. It was Ann.

"How was your day?"

Typical of Ann—and how wise she was not to ask "how are you?" She knew it was not good.

"She's dead. She's dead and I can't believe it. You know it's true don't you Ann?"

In a flash, Ann was beside me, her arm around me, hugging, squeezing, and constantly reminding me of what I really needed.

"I'm afraid it's going to take a while for it to sink in," she said.

"She's dead, Ann," I repeated. "Gone forever. What happens now? To me? To Giles and me? To any and all of us? What happens tomorrow when I wake up and she's not there? Tell me, what am I going to do then? How am I going to begin to survive?"

I stood up and paced, my voice rising in panic. Ann let me ramble.

"No more phone calls—no asking for gas money—no more borrowing my clothes or shoes—no dishes in the sink—no arguments—no coming home in the middle of the night—no more tears—laughter—no bloody nothing."

I sat down again, buried my face in my hands and sobbed. Earth quaking, uncontrolled, inconsolable, howls of misery.

I stood up and threw the empty beer bottle as far as I could into the grass.

"It's not fair, Ann. Just as Megan was believing in herself—just as our relationship was getting better—her whole future lay before her, mapped out so carefully. She'd worked hard in school—she was a good Christian, practicing and planning. She truly, truly believed in God. How could He let this happen? I thought He was supposed to be all about love—I don't understand…"

I slumped back down on the hard bench.

"…At this particular moment, I really hate God." Spent, I was instantly ashamed.

"You've every right to be angry," said Ann. "I'm sure God understands, and I don't get it any more than you do. I think that when we die everything becomes clear to us then."

"Hell's teeth, Ann, I could live to be a hundred. Will He make me suffer that long? I wish I'd been in the car and died with Megan. I need explanations now, right now."

Another squeeze from my friend and sensible silence.

Off I went again.

"I might be able to understand it a bit more if she'd been sick with some long drawn out illness and needed to die to relieve the pain. But this, in the prime of her life, at peak fitness of mind, body and spirit—it's like some cruel joke. Or do you think maybe it's something I've done wrong in the past, and God is punishing me; because He sure as hell is doing that."

"No," said Ann. " I don't believe God is vindictive. I know this must be so hard for you, and wish I could help with a rationale, but we're all in the same boat, following by blind faith. Remember what Pastor Kevin said, that it was a good day for Megan, but a bad day for us. I firmly believe she's OK—that God had some special plan for her—she's free, she…"

"Hello."

Neither of us had seen or heard Giles approach.

"Sorry, I hope I'm not interrupting you two."

"No, no," said Ann before I could speak.

Giles came to my side and gently stroked my arm.

"How are you?" Without waiting for a reply, he continued. "I tried calling once or twice, but either you were out here or didn't want to answer."

"Both," I said, and wandered off to retrieve the thrown beer bottle, and thought about what Ann had just said to me. God is not vindictive. God is not cruel. God has a plan.

Bugger God and his plan.

I sulkily followed Ann and Giles inside.

"Come, show me where you keep the dog food," said Ann.

Together we fed Thatcher and Liza, my lovely dogs, grateful for the smallest scrap of attention, let alone food.

Ann didn't leave after one beer. Giles kept insisting she have another and then just one more. It became embarrassing, as though he was desperate not to be alone with me. Perhaps his misbehavior last night was out of a need to feel cared for or loved by someone else. Somebody other than me might carry more weight.

Paula?

Your paranoia is showing again.

Knowing Ann didn't want to be impolite, I could sense her discomfort. The final time she got up to go I stood up with her, and we said our good-byes at the door.

Right, Giles, talk to me. Let me help you. I'm your wife dammit.

We did talk. Inane, stupid, supercilious stuff. Megan's name wasn't mentioned once. He was overly excited about the upcoming weekend.

We must go forward. Keep busy.

The sour remnants of the previous night rose up in my mouth— *Keg of beer? Escorting my wife from our daughter's funeral? Shit. Don't start again.*

It was as if I were two people going into the bedroom with Giles that night. The first, a capable woman, dealing with the greatest tragedy of all time—the death of her child. In the light of such profound shock, coping "splendidly" with arrangements of church, High School, hospital and such. Graciously acknowledging the literally thousands of people who had paid respects, sensitive to the needs of everyone. The very face of dignity and decorum.

The second, a shadow—a crumpled soul desperate for suspension of sense and consciousness, an angry mind churning with questions. All the same. Why? Why? Why? With no answers, and shattered expectations of God, a body, yearning for love and tenderness and supplication. A face of despair.

Chapter Sixteen

We raced down the I4, very late to catch our plane. I was driving because I always could drive faster than Giles. Although we were going against traffic, rush hour was still ridiculous. Giles and his constant need to always delay leaving his damn office.

"C'mon, move." The gap in the road meant we could reach at least 45mph.

"Go easy," said Giles. "We don't want to get a ticket."

"Giles, the last thing I want right now is to miss that flight and spend hours waiting for the next one. Not to mention Wendy and Vincent will be there to pick us up in Atlanta."

"OK. OK. but slow down a bit."

"This bloody traffic is forcing me to."

At last, Orlando airport, screech to a halt, fumble for the parking pass, quick, there's a space, remember to lock the car doors and run. This time Giles was faster than me and grabbed my suitcase and the five-pound ham I was carrying. Another ham from the abundant supply of food at our house had gone into the freezer for a later date.

"Go ahead," I told him. "See if you can't hold the plane for me." I grinned at the thought of Giles standing on the tarmac waving his arms at a taxiing plane. Wait wait.

He was gone.

I eventually arrived at the gate panting and disheveled only to have Giles tell me the flight was delayed due to bad weather north of us. Great, all that rushing to hurry up and wait. I flopped into a seat to calm my breathing and adjust my heart rate.

After a while I looked around and wondered about the people sitting in the surrounding area with us.

Over there, an older couple, probably not frequent fliers. The wife had a nervous little twitch at the corner of her mouth, and her husband constantly checked his bag for something or other. I guessed they were going to visit their daughter and grandchildren.

Your children would have been dark haired like you Megan, whoever you married. Megan married? I couldn't imagine it.

I smiled to myself, a wry smile, as I remembered one of Giles's friends telling her, one day, she would make someone a wonderful ex-wife. It had seemed cruel to me at the time, although I'd laughed with the others. Megan was such a feisty, independent individual; no one would or could have tamed her.

Now look at this smart man reading his Time magazine. A true ruddy-faced cowboy. He was wearing a beautifully starched, cream shirt with epaulets and pleated pockets. The matching trousers had creases so sharp they could have sliced bread, and his dress boots had a shine to dazzle. Even his Stetson hat was the color of Jersey cow milk. He'd obviously spent time scrubbing his hands, but couldn't quite get the working fingernails completely free of dirt. And where was his horse?

I shamelessly stared at him, and fancied Megan would have been fascinated by this man, and struck up a conversation with him—asked him all sorts of questions causing him to smile. No matter how short the duration of their meeting, he would not soon have forgotten her.

'Flight … non stop to Atlanta now boarding at gate…'

Giles nudged me, picked up the bags and guided me on board. We took our seats at the very back of the plane and prepared for take off. Helen had bought three little crystal angel pins, one each for herself, Gail and me to wear at the memorial service. I wore this meaningful symbol on my collar and caressed it constantly as the plane hurtled down the runway.

Fly with me Megan.

Giles was holding my hand. I looked down and noticed the hairs below his knuckles, once, fiery red faded now with age. The ginger gene that had given Megan's hair glorious auburn highlights. I felt a prickling, burning sensation in my eyes. I blinked hard and stared up to the ceiling, but could not halt the steady trickle of tears running down my face. Giles raised the armrest between us and put his arm around me. Nothing was said, but the comfort he gave me in that small gesture was enough.

It was a bumpy two-hour flight, but it didn't worry me. I was beyond caring whether I lived or died. Maybe the consolatory actions afforded me by my husband relieved my fear, either of dying, or worse, living.

We didn't talk much, and before long were on the ground again, walking to meet our friends.

For me, the forty-minute journey back to their house passed in a blur of oncoming horizontal car lights. I looked out into the black night and spoke very little, even then in monosyllables. Thank goodness our hosts respected my silence as I was beginning to wonder if we'd done the right thing by coming. I had no energy to communicate; I wanted to withdraw within. Giles chatted on. Mostly about business or the running group's activities. I heard that a lot of the friends we knew when we'd lived in Georgia years before were looking forward to seeing us tomorrow at the run.

The booming, baritone bark of Vince's harlequin Great Dane, Kitty could be heard from inside the house. The moment the garage door to the kitchen was opened, she bounded through to greet friend or foe alike. Thank God for Kitty. All focus and attention was on her, easing tension and making the transition within, a sloppy, boisterous affair.

Wendy took us to our room, and my heart sank. Two single beds. What had happened to the big comfortable double we'd slept in, on our many trips to Atlanta?

Disguising my disappointment, I managed, "Oh, you've changed things around."

"Yes," said Wendy. "It's much better for non-married couples this way."

So, I suppose I'm a non-married now.

Giles on the other hand seemed to perk up. He was in a very good mood, laughing a lot, albeit mostly at his own little jokes, but no matter. He became overly attentive, constantly touching me, giving me small pecks on the cheek, or asking about my well-being. Maybe he was overjoyed at not having to sleep in the same bed with me, I didn't know. But with the pressure off, he was relaxed and solicitous. I loved him like this, and eagerly responded, for the time being forgetting all past hurts and mistakes.

We were amongst friends and were going to see more tomorrow. Most of them we had met on St. Simon's Island during a family holiday many years ago. Megan was nine, and even at that age, I well remember how effortlessly she interacted with people three times her age, and often beat them running.

Vincent made thick ham and mustard sandwiches, which we ate on the back porch under a canopy of sweet smelling wisteria. Glimpses of the crystal clear night beyond became visible through gaps made by the soft, barely discernible breeze. After a couple of

German beers and easy conversation, quick witticisms from Wendy, light banter from Vince, we were all relaxed. It was positively idyllic, except for one thing...

"C'mon," said Giles. "Time for bed."

Almost asleep, I bade goodnight to our hosts and with my husband's help, staggered to our room.

"Clean my teeth for me, Giles. I'm too tired."

He laughed.

"Come, I'll help you. Where's your brush?"

I'd forgotten it, and my nightie. Wendy provided both, and I made a mental note to always have a new toothbrush on hand for any future visitors of my own.

Giles tucked me into bed. He knelt by my side, hugged and kissed me, and almost told me he loved me. I could feel it in the snuggle. I sensed the urge and remembered the habit, but refused to prompt him.

Say it, God damn you, say it. Bloody hell. If we were in one bed...

"Good night."

Lay your head upon my pillow,

Hold your warm and tender body close to mine...

"Good night."

...for the good times.

I woke with a start. Where was I? It was still dark and it took me a moment to realize I was not in my own bed, nor at home. I could hear Giles's breathing, nasal but steady. I would have liked to have slept longer, but once my eyes were open, I knew more sleep was impossible. I crept out of the bedroom and in the glow of a night-light, luckily spotted Kitty sprawled over the entire space of the hallway. She raised her head to look at me, wagged the tip of her tail and indicated this was her space and she had not the slightest intention of moving. I stepped between her legs and made my way to the kitchen.

To my surprise, I saw Wendy in the breakfast nook, wearing purple pajamas, her long dark hair free from the customary topknot style. She was drinking coffee and reading the morning paper.

"Couldn't sleep?" she asked when she saw me.

"Not any more," I replied. "But what about you? Did you even go to bed?"

She chuckled. "Oh yes. I don't need much sleep and I'm always up this early. It's the best time of the day. Would you like some coffee?"

"I'd prefer tea. But sit still, I can make it myself."

I sat opposite Wendy and it was lovely. Just the two of us—quiet—peaceful, with the dawning light of the new day beginning to appear through the open curtainless window. Birds were cranking up, and the combined aromas of wisteria and jasmine from the porch drifted in.

Gently, Wendy put her hand over mine. "I'm so sorry about Megan. I can't imagine what you're going through. I've never been fortunate enough to have been blessed with a child, but I do know Megan was so beautiful and a wonderful credit to you and Giles."

I looked at her and tears welled up in my eyes.

"Thanks, Wendy. Deep inside I know she's gone, but right now it's not real. I keep thinking I'll wake up tomorrow or next week and it'll all be a dream. Giles seems to be going on normally, but I can't. I don't want to do anything—every task is an ordeal and I—I –" I shrugged my shoulders. "I just don't care."

"Give yourself time," said Wendy. "I know it's an old cliché, but time does heal. It's hard to believe right now; your loss is so great."

I nodded my agreement.

"Besides," Wendy continued. "Don't forget men and women

grieve differently. Men generally put on a bold face and see tears as a weakness. You know, no use crying now—we must go forward etc., etc., and I see Giles with that stiff British upper lip mentality."

"That's true," I said. "He won't let me in. I've no idea how he really feels, and to tell you the truth, I've yet to see him shed a tear. He's gone back to work and wants me to return to school next week. But I can't. How can I concentrate? And somehow it would seem sacrilegious—as if I didn't really love her enough or care that she's dead—or God forbid, that she existed at all." Tears ran freely down my face now and I grabbed a paper napkin from the stack in the middle of the table to hastily mop the flow.

"Stop," said Wendy, sharply, both her hands on mine now. "You must not do this to yourself. You must do things and live your life in your own way at your own pace. Don't let anyone tell you what to do or how to grieve. Your heart is breaking for Megan. Nobody knows how you feel, except maybe the other girl who died's mother. You must take all the time in the world to recover."

"I don't think I ever will."

Vince joined us as cheerful as he was the night before.

"Did you bring your running shoes? It's going to be a sunny day and I expect a good turn out at the run. Where's that loafing husband of yours, isn't he up yet? Shall I send Kitty in to wake him?"

Kitty stood looking at Vince, furiously wagged her tail, excited at the prospect of a good prank.

Thanks Vince for normalization. And if you saw my tears, thanks for not mentioning it.

"No need." Giles came into the kitchen and bent to stroke the dog. "Sorry, Kitty, to do you out of some mischief. How is everyone this fine morning?" He came towards me and kissed me. "And how are you? Did you sleep?"

"A little," I answered.

Great, he's still in a good mood. I can lean on him today.

"Ham and eggs for breakfast?" Vince was already at the open refrigerator, generously helping himself to previously cut chunks of meat.

"If there's any left," quipped, Wendy. And so continued the light bantering, goodwill and company of the night before.

"Who's for a Bloody Mary?"

Fantastic. Just what I need.

On the way to the start of the run, I thought back several years, to one of the countless games we played as a family on long tedious car journeys. Megan was ten.

I spy with my little eye, something beginning with G.

Grass? No. Gate? No. Green trees? No. Garbage? No. Gum tree? (Giles) No. Gentleman? (Me) That floored her for a minute. No.

Ten miles further on—Come on Megan, we give up. GOAT! Goat? Goat? Where the heck is a goat? Back there in a field. Ay ay ay! She hated to lose.

"Hello, how nice to see you again—Sorry to hear about Megan— How are you?—Haven't seen you in a while."

People, some of whom I instantly recognized, others whose faces were familiar and some I had trouble putting names to, surrounded us. Fortunately Giles did most of the talking; he was in his element— like a prodigal son, embracing, engaging, and graciously answering question after question. He greeted everyone with palpable enthusiasm that I thought by sheer osmosis I ought to be able to absorb some of his strength. I was a young blushing bride, a proud mother of his children, a special confidante, friend and lover. I was safe by his side, a lifetime of memories secure within our marriage. He was constantly with me and I loved him for that.

I didn't run but walked a shortened course with the fair, the fat and the injured.

It was odd that I felt slightly embarrassed at first and couldn't meet anyone's eye, (*why do I feel like that? I've done nothing wrong*) but after the initial "sorries" I fell into step with old and new friends alike. Wendy was the go between, steering them and me to either talk about Megan or not. She was in control and my protector. For the first time since Megan's death I felt somewhat at ease. This group wasn't about me or Giles or Megan. It was a relief not to be the center of attention, yet in a weird way I wanted to shout out "don't forget about Megan". I had to keep my daughter first and foremost at everyone else's center, lest she be forgotten.

Who is Megan?

A few favorite friends, Wendy and Vince, Giles and I adjourned to the local pub for lunch after the run. It was a spit and sawdust place, sparsely inhabited on that early Saturday afternoon. I didn't want to eat, especially greasy fried food, but there wasn't much choice. I sat quietly between Dave and Giles as they chowed down on hamburgers. I sipped my beer and occasionally stole a French fry from both plates. Another beer and I was hungry, another and I smiled, another and I was laughing at their jokes, the guilty conscience of normality stalled for a while. Ron couldn't help himself he was very funny, and Mark, usually so dour, surpassed himself with one-liners. After an hour it was as though we'd never left Atlanta, and after two I was sorry everyone had to leave, but then some of them were coming to Wendy's house for Sunday lunch the next day.

We all took a nap the minute we arrived home. I surprised myself by sleeping, something I didn't or couldn't normally do during the day, no matter how hard I tried.

I awoke to find Giles staring at me from his bed on the other side of the room.

"Hi. How do you feel?"

"Fine, thanks," I replied. *How long had he'd been looking at me like that?*

"Actually quite refreshed. It was great seeing such old friends. I hadn't realized how much I missed them, or how much they thought of Megan."

"Yes, well, most of them knew her from way back and watched her grow up. I was talking to Dave and some others, and I thought we might have a sort of memorial run for Megan when we get back to Orlando. Invite our friends from here and Alabama and all the old-timers that we don't see so much of these days. People like Phil Carpenter and Barry Waite for example. What do you think?"

"Good idea." I sat on the side of my bed and looked straight into Giles's eyes. "But, I will tell you this to your face, I will not tolerate those awful girls, Jodie and the other one, whatshername Dawn? Margie? You know whom I mean. They seem to hang around every time there's a run with free beer." I was deliberately careful not to mention Paula.

"They're harmless, and only showing support for me."

"They're obnoxious, and this has nothing to do with me being jealous or whatever. I just feel they're rude and crude and out for what they can get. They didn't know Megan, and they certainly don't know me and I won't ever have them in my house again."

Mask like, Giles stared back at me and said not a word. In an instant he was out of bed.

"What's planned for tonight? Do you know?"

Drop it. Don't go any further. You know this is typical of him to abruptly change the subject to evade anything he doesn't want to talk about.

I wisely heeded my own advice.

"I think Wendy was going to make supper and suggested we play cards. I'd like that—just like old times."

This is exactly what we did. Always a good host, in early spring Atlanta, Vince lit a fire to ward off the chill. Kitty thought this was made especially for her as she promptly plonked herself in front of it. We consumed ham and cheese frittatas with a simple spinach and mushroom salad and washed it down with Italian wine and English cider. Old favorites, Willie Nelson, Waylon Jennings and Jimmy Buffet kept our feet tapping while we shuffled the cards. We played canasta; first the girls against the boys and later Vince and I paired against Giles and Wendy. We laughed a lot and we reminisced a lot, and Giles was as sweet and attentive, as I'd ever known him. At the end of a wonderful evening with civilized genteel company, Vince raised his glass.

"To Megan."

"To Megan." We chorused.

Again as I woke I wondered where I was. There was something about sleeping in a twin bed that wasn't quite right, not big enough to stretch either way. But it was daylight so I must have slept some. Giles was gone from his bed and I was surprised I hadn't heard him leave. It was quiet, and I lay for a while thinking about the nightmare we'd been through, and how it was like a million years ago and then again two seconds since. Would I ever be able to come to terms with it? Would I ever be able to relax and laugh and feel comfortable? Would there ever be a second I didn't think about Megan? She was wrapped around my heart and continued to beat out her rhythm with my own.

Bridget, my long since dead mother-in-law, suddenly popped into my head. She and I had had a cordial relationship; I considered myself a dutiful daughter-in-law, and she was definitely a noninterfering mother-in-law. Anyway, being oceans apart (literally), we hadn't seen too much of each other to be upset or get on each other's nerves. Her only daughter, Giles's older sister, had drowned at sea when she was eighteen. This happened within a year of Bridget's husband's tragic early death of a stroke, and as much as I would respectfully encourage Biddy to talk about Shirley or Hamilton, she never did. Yes, there were monosyllables here and there to answer my questions, but no heartfelt outpourings. Giles was only six when his Dad died and barely remembers Shirley for teaching him how to swim.

We have something in common now Biddy. I know how you must have felt. Did you mourn your daughter's death more than your husband's? That's a terrible question. Would I feel like I do now if Giles had died instead of Megan?

Giles appeared with two cups of tea in hand.

"You're awake at last. You had a good sleep."

"I suppose I did. What time is it?"

"Almost nine."

"What! I don't believe it."

Giles laughed and sat on the side of my bed.

"You obviously needed the rest and I hadn't the heart to wake you. Do you feel better?"

Funny that, I didn't know grief was an illness. Giles is so simple—rest and sleep are a "cure". Stoppit! He's trying to be nice, don't be cruel.

"Yes," I said. "Much." *Good girl, leave it at that.*

"If you don't mind, I'm going for a quick run with Vince."

"Sure," I replied. "I don't mind at all, and anyway I must get up and help Wendy. I think she said there were about twenty people coming to lunch. Remind me again what time our flight is tonight."

"Sixish. We have to leave here by four." He leaned towards me and kissed me, a brief, familiar kiss between husband and wife. "See you later."

I lay back against the pillows and pondered. I'd had enough. I wished I were home with Roger. For a cat, he certainly gave me the solace I craved, better than any human did. I didn't want to see any more people, I didn't want to be socially nice and I was sick of everyone saying how sorry they were. What were they sorry about? It all seemed so contrived; yet, in my heart I knew some of them were genuinely sad for either Megan or me or both. And I also knew that I must not be rude.

Shit! Double, triple, whipple, dipple, shit. All the despair was rising to the surface like scum on boiling tripe. I was alone in a well-meaning crowd, utterly isolated in the agony of maternal grief. I was so angry my teeth were clenched shut and my hands tight fists.

Get up, you stupid fool. You can't stay here all day. You have to keep going.

Slowly, without interest, I dressed for the day.

In the past I'd never really taken to her. She had that high and mighty attorney aloofness with the ability to make me feel inferior. I was glad when she moved to Atlanta and I didn't have to deal with her anymore. Now as she lumbered towards me I struggled to remember her name.

"Hey, Nicky, do you want another drink?"

I looked beyond her to see a handsome, dark haired man waving an empty glass in the air.

"Thanks," she nodded.

And thanks to you, whoever you are.

Nicola. A name I always thought didn't suit this big-boned, brassy woman with crooked teeth. Couldn't she afford to have them fixed? Nicola-s should be petite, quiet, perfectly mannered young ladies with no physical faults.

"Hello."

"Hello, Nicky! How are you?"

"Fine. I was sorry to hear about Megan. She had balls, that girl."

Yes, she did, but I wish you hadn't said it quite like that.

The good-looking man joined us with two glasses in hand.

"This is my husband, George. I don't think you ever met him."

We shook hands.

"No," I said. " I would have remembered you." I hoped dear Nicky caught the irony in my voice. When single, she had frequently tried hitting on Giles and feigned dismay when he showed no interest in her. I never knew whether she was for real or playing. Again that attorney mentality.

"I'm sorry for your loss," George said. "She sounded like a great girl. I wish I could have known her."

"Thanks." I didn't know what else to say to him. Just leave me to stare at his enormously attractive face.

"Can I get you a drink?"

"No thanks," I told him. "I'm OK for right now." Giles, I need some help.

As if by magic Giles appeared by my side.

"Hey there. How's everyone doing? Nice to see you again George."

How did Giles know George and I didn't?

The two men engaged in conversation, which left me with Nicola. There was a horrible silence until we both started to talk at once.

"You first," I prompted.

"What I was going to say is that I'm working in corporate law now which involves all kinds of different aspects. I was wondering if you had any kind of insurance on Megan?"

"Sure," I replied. "State Farm has just given us a substantial cheque."

"That's quite normal," said Nicky. "But did you know there's a lot more to be had?"

"Really? From whom? I'm not interested in suing anyone."

"No, you don't understand. Most insurance companies pay out the initial amount knowing it's quite generous for most people. And it is. It's paid out in the first week during the most emotional time after the death of a loved one. They're hoping that's all they have to do, and usually it is, as the majority of people either don't understand the law or are in ignorance of further possibilities." Nicky sipped her drink.

Crikey! Look at that diamond.

"You're right I don't understand," I said. "I'll say again that I'm adamant about not suing Heather's family. They, like us, have suffered enough in what I truly believe was a pure accident."

Nicky laid her hand on my arm and tightened her grip in an almost conspiratorial way.

"Heather's family won't know anything about it. You won't be suing Heather; you'll be going after her insurance company. They owe you. That's what you pay insurance for."

Nicky must have seen the skeptical look on my face as she pushed her point further.

"I can assure you Heather's family will not be involved, they will not even know you've done anything. Their insurance premiums will not be affected. This is money due to you that usually goes unclaimed. Please tell me you'll think about it, and if you have any questions call me, Giles has my number."

Yes he does.

"When you get back to Orlando, ask Carl to give you the name of his attorney. I know he'll be able to help you."

"Thanks. I will think about it, and talk it over with Giles."

We slowly integrated back into the small crowd gathered on the porch. A couple in their late thirties stood in the middle cooing over their newly adopted Chinese baby. I wished them all the best. Others I hadn't seen for a long time talked briefly. It was a bit awkward; nobody really knew what to say to me. I was bored; I was tired; I was fed up; the strain of putting on a brave face loathsome and my heart heavy from trivial socializing. Four o'clock couldn't come soon enough for me.

We had Sam in the car with us on the return journey to the airport. His plane left more or less at the same time as ours. Nice guy, known him for years, but I didn't have another word to say to him now. Just as well Vince and Giles did all the talking; they didn't need me. *Now there's a daunting thought; who does?*

Need. To be necessary. Some necessity of thought or action. An obligation. A circumstance requiring some course. Helen and Gail needed me, but could manage without me at a push. Liza, Thatcher and Roger needed me; there's some comfort in that. But did Giles? Was he going to stay with me tonight? A few days ago I felt he wanted to move back into his apartment. Was I to be dismissed when I needed to be needed? I thoroughly depressed myself with these maudlin thoughts for the remaining minutes of the trip.

Somebody turned the light off. We were back in Orlando and Giles had reverted to that place where I couldn't reach him. He'd been so gentle and caring and wonderful during the last few days, but now, on the way home on the darkened interstate highway, we spoke in single monotonic words and I sensed the gap widening once more.

"Please stay with me tonight," I blurted out, unable to bear the uncertainty any longer.

"If you'd like me to."

The rush of dogs was marvelous. Dear Liza and Thatcher were overjoyed to see us. It was so good to be home. Thank God for the animals, because like Kitty in Atlanta, who had made an awkward situation there more comfortable, ours made the transition into a very black, deathly quiet house almost bearable.

Lights on, kitchen door to the garage left open so the dogs could continue to mingle around our ankles, familiar smells peculiar to one's own family and cooking, and a tidy kitchen. Ann must have done this, bless her. Welcome home, the note said.

"Tea?" asked Giles.

"Yes, that sounds good, thanks."

I looked around for Roger whom I missed more than anything. I'd been gone barely two days.

It was our habit to walk the dogs down the lane before bed, so we took our tea and sauntered, Thatcher close to my side instead of his usual race to the finish line.

I told Giles of my conversation with Nicola that afternoon.

"What do you think?"

"No, I'm not interested," he said. "That's the trouble with America, everyone suing everyone else."

"This is slightly different," I ventured. "Like you, I'm not interested in suing anyone personally. I would never do that to Heather's family. But Nicola told me we'd be claiming what is rightfully ours from Heather's car insurance company. I can't see what's wrong with that."

"OK. I still think it's a waste of time, but do what you want. You will anyway."

"There's no need to be nasty about this. Nicky only told me about these possibilities today and I'm looking for your input—a discussion rather than an argument. I know nothing of legal matters or insurance claims so let me do a little more research. I'll call Carl in the morning, Nicky seems to think he'll be able to help."

"Fine."

Shut down, melt down, call it what you'd like, this conversation is over.

"Meow, meow, meow."

"Hey, Rog." Tail straight up in the air, and talking all the way, Roger came waddling towards us. I picked him up before Thatcher could bowl him over in playful jealousy. I nuzzled my face into his.

"I missed you Roger." But he struggled, jumped free of my arms and ran off with Thatcher in hot pursuit.

You little wretch, I know I've been gone, but you can't give me too much too soon can you.

There was no question of sex when we went to bed that night. Giles's body language told me everything; the bubble had burst. I was back to square one, battling his demons and more of my own. I actually felt nothing, I couldn't be bothered to feel, and I hadn't the energy to try. Sleep didn't come easy either; I tossed and turned, and eventually lay on my back, eyes wide open.

You should be ashamed of yourself at a time like this, thinking of sex. I just wanted to be loved. I wanted to be held. I wanted to feel the closeness of another body next to mine, as one, not with his back to me snoring in oblivion. I'm so scared; what is going to happen to me? Am I destined to be on my own? Why do I feel such rejection? Megan, please help me.

Tears of self-pity ran over my cheeks and trickled behind my ears. I sniffed. I was frightened Giles would wake. Worse, I feared he would wake and be angry with me.

"For God's sake," he would say. "Just go to sleep."

That's a bit pathetic, to be frightened of your own husband.

I slithered out of bed debating whether to call Helen. The Chicago time zone put her an hour behind, but still it was late. I should have called earlier to let her know we were home. It was definitely too late to call Gail. And what would I say? I wanted to have sex with your father but he deplored the notion. Rejected it out of sight no less.

I don't think so.

I switched the television on in the sitting room. I hadn't seen or heard news for days. Nothing interested me and I began to idly flip channels. Settling for a re-run of "I love Lucy" with the sound turned low; I stretched out on the couch and closed my eyes.

Quick Giles. Bring the knife. Quick, the bloody thing has got her. I stayed in the boat with my mother and watched my father dive into the freezing cold water.

She only had five hundred yards to swim to safety but the shark was faster, and in a flurry of flesh and blood we watched in horror as Megan struggled for life. As her head re-appeared she was smiling and the grin got bigger and wider. I'm OK, this is fun, and she heaved herself into the boat profusely bleeding from a two foot gash in her side but then again, seemingly unhurt. God it was cold...

I woke, chilled to the bone and breathing fast. I don't remember my father being able to swim; in fact I couldn't ever recall seeing him in the ocean, or even yet in a swimsuit. And as for my mother, she hated boats and water. It was as much as I could do to get her on the English Channel ferry on her only trip to Europe many years ago. I had family photographs taken at the seaside when we were kids, my father in a collar and tie, my mother in a blouse and skirt and stockings!

What did it all mean? Were my long dead parents united with Megan? Were they taking care of her? The shark, and the gash? There must be a symbolic meaning there.

I roused myself only to turn the TV off and crawl back into bed with Giles. The warmth was amazing and I shifted as close as I dared without waking him. And I slept—a lovely, deep dreamless sleep.

I didn't remember the dream until much later the next day when a shiver swept my body. "Somebody walking over your grave" my mother used to say. I wished it were true.

Giles had gone off to work with hardly a word, seemingly in haste, and without breakfast. He'd taken his weekend bag and toiletries, so I knew he wouldn't be back to the house that night. I was expecting this but didn't know what to say to him. Now, mid-morning, despair was setting in once more. Alone, panicky alone, I wandered in and out of the house.

Oh my God, what am I going to do?

I couldn't stop the tears starting up. I couldn't stop them.

Megan, my darling girl, will it always be like this?

The telephone rang, jolting me out of my chair.

"This is Betty. How are you?"

"O.K. I suppose. Well not really—" My school teacher was the last person I expected to call me at that time.

"I know how you feel," Betty said. "When I lost my grandfather I was sad for the longest time. But you know the best thing you should do is come back to school. We all miss you and I feel it would be better for you to keep your mind occupied. I'm sure this is what Megan would wish for you. She would want you to get on with your life. Actually, I was expecting you this morning and don't want you to get too far behind."

"I can't, Betty. It's too soon—I can't concentrate—I'm a mess—"

Again she interrupted me.

"Come back soon. I know this is the best way."

"I'll think about it—maybe next week. Sorry, Betty I have to go now, but thanks for your good wishes and advice. 'Bye"

Now I was angry. How did she know how I feel? She's never lost a daughter. Grandfathers are supposed to die in old age, that's the natural law. How does she presume to know what's best for me?

And how dare she tell me what Megan would want. I don't want to occupy my mind. I want to fill that space with grief. Forever and ever and ever. I don't care if I never go back to school; she can't tell me what to do.

And I cried harder.

The telephone rang constantly after Betty's call, but not one of them was from Giles. I guessed he was too busy, and anyway life was back to normal. Right?

I could hardly speak I was so depressed and only answered the phone when I wanted to. One of the calls I should have taken was from my brother, Michael in England, but as I guiltily listened to his message on the machine, so full of love and compassion, I was glad I didn't. It seemed everything and everyone made me cry. If someone called or if they didn't. If they said kind words or merely wanted an appointment to see my house. And why are the birds so bloody cheerful?

Please, Liza, stop barking at nothing.

Leave me alone.

No, don't.

I was emotionally flat lining. My heart couldn't take any more, my brain lifeless and I was spinning out of control. Tears needed no effort on my part to fall free.

Help, help, help.

Do something before you go under completely.

Chapter Seventeen

I walked the dogs down the lane. Slowly and deliberately I breathed deep chunks of air so that I returned to the house, still depressed but somewhat calmer.

There was a message from Giles.

Wouldn't you know he would call the minute you left the house?

He probably ought to go back to his apartment tonight (I knew that) and he would talk to me later.

I stared at the phone and remembered when we first came to America how I stayed close to it expecting the return call that never came. "Later"—a flippant brush off.

After an hour of doing nothing, I pulled myself together enough to call Carl. I surmised he'd be out patrolling somewhere, so left a message to call me, later!

More painful stagnant hours followed that I couldn't remember and probably were best forgotten anyway, I walked Thatcher and Liza again, (*they must be very confused*) fed them, showered and climbed into bed. It was six o'clock.

Twilight. It was getting dark outside and I purposely left the curtains open and all lights off. I loved that time of day when tree silhouettes became velvet black against a reddening sky, and with each passing minute there was promise of moonlight and stars.

Night creatures stirred, a frog croaked, a bobwhite called and for a second or two I imagined I was back in Africa…

"Are you all right?"

It was Giles, and I must have automatically answered the phone.

"Sorry. Were you sleeping?"

"No, just dozing, and yes, I'm OK thanks." I caught sight of the luminous hands of the bedside clock. It was twenty minutes to nine.

"I'm still at work," Giles continued. "But I'm planning to finish up here shortly and head back to my apartment (*didn't I know it*) if that's all right with you."

"Fine." I bleated in a whisper.

"Sorry, what was that? I couldn't hear you?"

"Yes, that's fine," I said louder and trying so hard to control the disappointment in my voice. Whether Giles noticed or not, I couldn't tell, but I knew the inevitability of his return to "normal" couldn't be put off any longer.

"I'll call you tomorrow. Good night."

I put the phone back in its cradle.

"Good night." I said out loud to the ceiling, fighting back tears. "Good night, good night—so formal and final and horrible. What am I, a bloody client? God, give me strength."

I headed for the kitchen, turning lights on in my path. There was a chill in the air, and I shivered slightly as my bare feet touched the stone tiled floor. What did I want? Tea? Beer? Simple decisions eluded me. I knew I wasn't handling myself well, with lack of self-confidence growing at an alarming rate. I must stop crying. I settled for water, pure, clean, cold water straight from the bottle—great.

There was nothing else to do but go back to bed. I tried reading for a while, but after I'd read the same paragraph over and over again, the National Geographic magazine held no interest for me. Television screamed frivolous nonsense and endless advertisements. I quickly switched it off and resumed what was fast becoming a normal stance for me, that of staring at the ceiling and watching the continuous rotations of the overhead fan. Sooner or later I would have to sort out Megan's clothes, tidy her room and dispose of the things most precious to her. I was fiercely adamant that no one but me would touch any of it—but I'll think about that tomorrow or tomorrow or maybe even...

The next day dawned grey with suffocating humidity. Before long, rain started, misty drizzle, reminding me of England. But this was Florida and rain rarely fell in the morning. I liked the rain, which usually energized me, but today I woke with a dull, pounding headache developing over both eyes. I must eat something, but after all the food that was in the house a week ago, it was hard to believe the cupboards were now sparse, the refrigerator almost empty of anything immediately edible. I found some cereal in the freezer, which I ate straight from the box, carelessly dropping crumbs as I wandered through the house without any determination of my next move.

Of course the phone rang. It was Carl.

"Good morning. I got your message late last night. How are you? Did you have a good trip to Atlanta? How are Wendy and Vince?"

I'd forgotten Carl also knew them.

"They're great, and it was a very good trip thanks, Carl. I had my doubts about going, but it was good for me to get away—hard coming back—but I'll be fine. Nicky, you remember her don't you? Big girl—blonde—full of herself—big shot attorney now."

"Always shooting her mouth off, very opinionated—yes I remember her all right."

I couldn't help grinning.

"Well, she says hello, and to ask you about an attorney you know here in Orlando who might be able to help me with an insurance claim?"

"Sure. His name is—I'll have to give you his number later, or you can look it up in the book. He's a great guy—did a superb job for me after my accident, and fast. I know he'll be able to help you—mention my name if you want. Uh-oh—I hear my radio going off. Duty calls—gotta go—love ya honey. I'll call you soon. 'Bye."

"Thanks for everything, Carl. 'Bye."

I love this man. We didn't know him when he had his serious accident, (he was hit by a passing car when he was booking a speeder) but I wished I could have helped him then as much as he's assisting us now.

Just that brief talk with Carl cheered me up. My headache still throbbed, but I felt a force activate within me; certainly enough to move me to shower and dress. I had to go to the grocery store. I needed to do something easy, something routine, something normal.

"How are you today?"

"Fine, thanks."

Fine? Fine? Your baby's dead and you answer" fine". What's with that?

Well, can you imagine if I'd held up the line by telling the grocery store cashier what had had happened to me in the last two weeks.

I paid my bill and scarpered out of the store. My head was swimming with normality.

Put the key in the lock—turn the engine over---foot off the brake—on the gas pedal—go. Hell's teeth I'm a schizophrenic—two people, with enough dread in my heart for four.

That little trip was a panic attack; I couldn't wait to get home.

It was raining quite hard as I parked the car and began to unload the groceries. My eyes were drawn upwards, to the sky where two dark grey clouds separated to reveal a bright shaft of sunlight. The image only lasted a moment or two, but it stopped me dead in my tracks. I felt instantly comforted, as though Megan was beaming down on me.

"It's OK, Mum," she seemed to say. "You're going to be all right. Time will heal everything."

The clouds came back together as one. In awe, I stared and stared, hoping for more, hoping for another revelation, but alas, the sky became darker and the rain continued to fall.

Megan's voice rang in my ears for the rest of the day.

You're going to be all right—you're going to be all right—you can do it—you can do it—remember the little engine that could.

Chapter Eighteen

And so the days on my own blended seamlessly into each other—no days—no nights—no routine. I answered the dwindling telephone calls, was polite and reverent. Ann called every day of course, as did Helen and Gail. Kathy (my school friend) kept me updated on hospital affairs, with plenty of urging to return to school. They all missed me. My friend, Scott from the funeral home dropped off the visitors' book from the memorial service. It was staggering to me to find out that over a thousand people were in the church that night. Megan had certainly left her mark, and what a wonderful tribute it was to her and us all.

One day, Matt Cooper's mother, Susan, made a splendid gesture by bringing lunch over, complete in a picnic basket. Simple tuna sandwiches on home made nutty bread, fresh fruit, and chocolate mint cookies, all washed down with a bottle of red wine. We talked of nothing but Megan, and oh how we laughed and cried, often at the same time. It was enough to keep me going for the rest of the day, and enough to put a smile back on my face at low points thereafter.

I ventured into Megan's room, but only stayed long enough to pick up a few discarded clothes and put them in the laundry basket. I needed a little more time to empty drawers and closets.

Giles told me of the pending visit from Jennifer's parents at the weekend. They were going to take all the girls' belongings left at my house, and her Dad was going to drive Heather's car back to Ohio. *Good, I'll be glad to see the back of that vehicle parked in the driveway.* Jennifer was still too sick to travel, but I couldn't summon enough courage to revisit her in hospital, a reminder that she was alive and would be whole again in time. She had her Mom with her—she'd be all right. The other two, Sarah and Julie had returned to their homes up north. They never called me, sadly; I probably would never see them again.

Saturday morning and Giles arrived unannounced.

"I thought you'd like to take the dogs for a long walk," he said.

Without much enthusiasm I nodded my assent.

"Would you like breakfast first?" I asked him.

"Just some toast would be fine, thanks."

"What time are Jennifer's parents coming?" I asked.

"Noon-ish they said, possibly early afternoon. Her father wants to get in at least four hours of driving in daylight. Shall we go?"

We drove a short distance in the country to a place where Giles knew we could let the dogs run free. It promised to be at least a five-mile hike. Thatcher was excited to be in the back of the truck and kept darting from side to side, often falling over Liza who stoically sat. Once we began our walk, I realized it was the best thing I could have done. It was wonderful to be in the open air. I could breathe, both physically and mentally and for the first time didn't feel stifled or completely overwhelmed with grief. We kept the conversation casual and focused for the main part on the flora and fauna of the bush. I loved to be with Giles like this; he was so nature knowledgeable and was always pointing out something of interest. It was nice—familiar—relaxed, and the exercise brought color to my cheeks and strength to my being. I reveled in watching

Thatcher dash hither and yon, nose down, and short stump of a tail constantly moving.

Lopping along behind us, "C'mon, Liza, good girl." For a dog with three legs, she kept up amazingly well.

We discussed going out the next day to look for houses, nothing too serious, just to drive around in a particular area to see what was out there. I kept silent that I longed to have a normal married life again. But the nagging feeling remained that I wanted it more than Giles did. I was always the one to bring up the subject of his moving back in with me. It was always my suggestions for our life ahead. I told everyone we were getting back together, never Giles. He rarely commented and when he did it was a grunt or a "maybe" or a "we'll talk about it later" and never did. For a brief time during our walk this morning, because we were in sync, I allowed myself to be lulled into thinking we had a bright future.

I hope this doesn't come back to haunt you for the blind fool you are.

Once back at home, like Cinderella after the Ball, the feeling of well-being vanished. I was back tippy-toeing on the ever present eggshell path.

I did not welcome the thought of visitors. However, when they came, Giles stepped up to the plate (*surprise*) and handled a difficult situation very well. We were all awkward in each other's company, but Giles busied himself with fetching suitcases from inside, offering tea, which was gratefully declined, and pointing out the nearest route to the I 75. Jennifer's Mom gushed platitudes; I must have helped her along with my sullen silence. Reason told me it wasn't her fault her child was alive and mine was dead, but my mind kept returning to the fact that if Jennifer had sat up front with her friend Heather, as she wanted to, then Megan would be in hospital now with broken legs, and she would be the one to make a full recovery and swim again and finish college and give me grandchildren and...

"You were very quiet."

"Yeah, well, I had nothing much to say." And I retreated from the driveway to the house, to my bedroom and began to change clothes. Giles watched me from the doorway.

"What would you like to do?"

"Nothing—I don't know—I hadn't given it any thought."

Giles was clearly trying, and I sensed getting frustrated at my non-compliance.

"Well—I think I'll go to the office and check any messages. Then I'll come and cook supper if you'd like; or we could go out to eat and watch a movie later? Maybe there's something good on TV or I could pick up a movie on the way back? What do you think?"

"Fine, whatever you want, it doesn't matter to me." I could feel I was about to cry again. "Just go, Giles. I need a little time to myself."

"You sure you're going to be OK?" He walked towards me, but I didn't give him an inch. I blew my nose and made for the bathroom.

"Don't worry about me, I'll be just fine."

What's the matter with you? Why the sarcastic tone? One minute you want Giles and the next, you don't. Poor guy, no wonder he's confused.

"Okay then, see you later." He was gone.

Then the real pity party began. I sat on the end of the bed and sulkily looked out of the window. I was sad, angry, confused, lonely and jealous; I missed Megan so much; nobody knew how I felt; nobody had any idea of the pain I was going through. I rocked back and forth with my hands over my eyes in a vain effort to stem the fresh flow of tears.

Why did this happen? I can't stand it.

I stood up and began to pace the floor crying freely now. I didn't bother wiping my nose or drying my eyes. On the floor now, down on my knees heaving with hysterical sobs, completely out of control. It was a fit of crying like I'd never had before, huge mournful lamentations and great howls of despair. I cried and cried until eventually I looked up to the ceiling and shouted.

"Look at me, God. Look at me. Do something. Help me please."

Within thirty seconds I stopped crying. It was a miracle, as though He had reached down and turned off the tap. I couldn't believe it.

The front doorbell rang. *God?* I got up and quickly dried my face and whipped a comb through my hair. From habit I suppose, I went to answer it, for God knows I must have still looked a mess, in spite of hasty repairs. When I opened the door a short, plump, balding man greeted me. *God?*

"Sorry to disturb you, but driving by I saw the For Sale sign in the yard. I don't have an appointment and wouldn't presume on you to show me your house, but could you tell me the asking price?"

When I told him, he said." That's a little out of my range, but thank you."

I felt he needed an explanation of my appearance so said to him. "Please excuse the way I look, but I've just had a death in the family. Otherwise I would have been happy to show you around."

"I'm sorry to hear that, and once again, sorry to disturb you. Goodbye."

"No problem. Goodbye." *Sorry, sorry, sorry—here we go again.* I watched him walk down the driveway thinking how easy it would be for any stranger to take advantage of me now in my fragile state. I wouldn't normally have opened the door without looking through the spy hole first. Was God looking out for me again in the space of five minutes? This man seemed perfectly decent but you never know when looks can be deceiving.

Another week went by just like the last one. I don't remember much of it, for most of the time I was on automatic pilot. Giles drifted in and out as he pleased, but never stayed overnight. For short periods of time I went to Megan's room, sat on the bed and gazed out of the window, devoid of feeling, all tears spent. I opened and closed drawers. I touched objects I knew were special to her that were now special to me. I did manage to wash her dirty clothes without any idea of what to do with them when clean. I did spontaneously cry, but never again like the massive attack I had while prostrate on the floor. A dull resignation took over, a solemn cloak of despair. I couldn't bring myself to go back to school although by now everyone was urging me to do so. I knew I couldn't put it off much longer or I would have to drop out. As I was three quarters of the way through the course, common sense prevailed and I conditioned myself to return the following Monday.

Chapter Nineteen

I was nervous entering the classroom, but it occurred to me that my teacher, Betty, would have pre-warned my classmates. There were only fourteen of us; welcome back, some said, but having said it I knew they felt uncomfortable. I hadn't been on vacation after all, and didn't know how to reply, so said nothing, merely inclined my head in acknowledgement. Others I wasn't so friendly with, wisely also said nothing. All the while, Kathy was as protective as a mother hen following after one of her chicks.

Betty gave a short matter-of-fact speech welcoming me back, downplaying any moroseness. The class resumed. I had to make up a few tests so was isolated to a desk in the back. Half way through a particularly difficult orthopedic exam, visions of Megan's many broken bones came to mind, and in sheer panic I had to get up and run out. The classroom was on the sixth floor and I stood by a long window in the hallway and looked out over downtown Orlando through a blur of tears. Betty was behind me in an instant.

"I can't do this," I blubbered. "It's too hard—I just can't get it together—I'm sorry if I've broken the rules of leaving the room during a test—I…"

Betty interrupted me. "I know it must be difficult for you. Take a little break here for a moment. Calm yourself."

I blew my nose, audibly took in a huge breath, closed my eyes and relaxed my shoulders.

"That's right. Take another breath like that, in through your nose and out through your mouth. Good. Would you like me to stay here with you?"

"I'm better now, thanks. I'll be all right."

"Give yourself a few more minutes and then come back and resume your test." She gently patted my shoulder. "I'm not worried about you leaving the room. You obviously weren't going to look up answers. You will get through this—take it one step at a time, just one baby step."

I nodded agreement although not fully trusting myself to believe this could be true.

Will there ever be a day when I'm not completely absorbed by this devastation?

The next day we were scheduled to return to the hospital to continue our clinical rotation. In the morning I somehow made it to the locker room, changed into scrubs and joined my fellow colleagues for orders of the day.

Please don't put me back in the heart room.

Memories of that fateful morning came flooding back as I struggled to maintain my composure. I was silently screaming—surgery, yes, but now it's me who needs to be sewn up—find a patch big enough to mend this broken heart. Impossible.

I joined my fellow students at the assignment board. Neuro! Oh no, Oh my God, I can't face messing about in someone's brain. I ran to the nurses' lounge, found an empty corner and buried my face in my hands. It's not easy seeing a stranger violently sobbing and I knew I must have been an embarrassment to everyone there. But, I couldn't stop and very shortly Betty was sitting beside me.

"Stop this."

"I can't."

"Yes, you can. Come on now, you must be strong. I'm not going to send you home. You have to start again, you have to go forward."

I sniffed and looked at her through my tears. I hated her at that moment. I hated her because I knew she was right and I hated her because she wouldn't indulge me.

"Please, Betty, don't put me in a neuro room. It's too much."

"All right. I must admit some of the neuro surgeons can be a bit rough—I need someone to go into the oocyte retrieval room. That shouldn't be too hard for you and the staff in there are all very nice."

Eggs. OK. I knew I couldn't complain about a second assignment and I had to go somewhere. Besides, I always wondered how they took eggs from an ovary and cultivated them outside the uterus in a petri dish.

It was fascinating for the first hour, but when you've seen one egg removed (slurped up in a glass straw) you've seen them all. The patient was not quite fully anesthetized, more in a dreamlike state, so, in a whisper to the doctor, I managed to ask a few appropriate questions but was soon bored and had to feign interest. I couldn't see myself as an ova collector for the rest of my career. In fact, I couldn't see the end of the day, nor yet the end of my training. Megan was constantly in my thoughts. It was so difficult to concentrate on anything else, but if I once didn't think about her for a moment, I was instantly overwhelmed with guilt.

I slogged through that first week back in school, like dragging my feet through molasses. I ate and slept poorly, didn't give a damn about my school homework, and even less about housework. All that penetrated was my friendship with Ann and the love I had for my animals. Without them I think I would have gone under. I saw nothing of Giles until the next weekend when we resumed our lukewarm attempt at house hunting.

Early one afternoon, I took a different way home from the hospital. No interstate. On a backstreet, I drove past a house with a huge neon sign in the window. Psychic. Cards Read by Dinah it said, Walk-ins Welcome. By sheer impulse I made a U-turn and parked outside an old wooden building that could have used a coat of paint. Up three rickety stairs and into a dimly lighted room, spare of furniture save a threadbare red velvet couch against one wall and incongruously, an enormous new Sony television blaring out cartoons in the opposite corner. The place smelled of incense, the overpowering sickly sweet smell favored by mystics. On top of the television was a bell. Ring for Service.

I felt a bit like Alice about to drop into the rabbit hole, when through a glass beaded curtain a woman appeared. She had long bleached blonde hair, jeans, a red tank top and gold flip-flops on her feet. It was difficult to determine her age; I first guessed middle thirties, but on closer inspection, smoker's lines around her mouth and the pallor of her skin, suggested late forties, maybe even fifty.

"Hello," I said. "Dinah?"

"Yes, dear."

"Is it possible to have a reading today?"

"Sure, honey. Come on in."

I bridled at "honey". I dislike syrupy endearments, but said nothing.

Dinah led me to a smaller room, just big enough for a table and two hard chairs, but brighter than the other and not nearly so smelly. She gave me the perfunctory disclaimer, absolving her of any right or wrong that might hint of the truth or not. The maybe's –the could be's—and the also ran's. I'd been to so called "psychics" before—it was all a game, but for twenty bucks and a half hour of my time—what the hell.

We got started with me shuffling and cutting the Tarot cards and Dinah dealing out the spread. It was all very routine—this was in my past—this means the stage you're in today—things to possibly come—all of which were horribly ambiguous and instantly forgettable. We talked a bit about "husband and children", again all predictable stuff.

After twenty or so minutes of this. "Could you tell me about my third daughter." I asked.

"Oh," said Dinah. "I only see her as a spirit."

With that, everything exploded. I put my hands to my face, mouth open, and stared at Dinah too dumbstruck to speak. She couldn't have possibly known that Megan had died, or even if she did, notwithstanding the copious news coverage, she couldn't have known I was her mother. I bore no identification anywhere, and Dinah didn't even know my first name.

The cards were put away. In the distance I heard a telephone ring—someone else must have answered. The bell on top of the television in the other room rang. Dinah ignored it. For the next two hours we talked. I told her all about Megan's life. I told her everything about the four girls' visit from Ohio for Spring Break and my uneasy feelings the morning of the accident. I told her about my mother and how she had died on the same day, ten years previously. I talked until spent, spilling out untold secrets and fearful feelings to this stranger who was one no more.

"Yes," Dinah said. "I know about Megan's death." She saw me frown.

"No," she continued, pressing forward and looking me straight in the eye. "I know about Megan's death, not from any newspaper cutting, but from knowing that her soul instantly left her and she's happy. She's gone from the crash site; she's at peace."

Hey, this is getting a bit spooky.

"On the other hand, her friend, Heather, is it? She's still trapped there and is desperately seeking a way out. Now there's a tormented soul, and you're the only one who can help her."

More spooky.

"Don't worry," said Dinah, seeing the look on my face. "You can do this. I will tell you what to do."

"What? How?"

Spooky beyond belief.

"Tonight when you get home, or maybe tomorrow would be better, as it's getting late. Anyway, when the sun is shining, I want you to go into Megan's room and call for Heather. Ask for Megan's help—she wants to help you. Then I want you to look out of the window up to the sky and say "I forgive you, Heather." Over and over again say it 'I forgive you Heather'. 'Go with Megan'. 'I forgive you'. Can you do that?"

C'mon, get me out of here.

"I'll try," I said, my voice little more than a whisper.

I don't remember the trip home. By divine guidance, my autonomy cells took over to drive the car to stop at red lights and keep to the speed limit. I felt wonderful—relaxed—in a way I hadn't felt since Megan had died. It was almost as if I were outside my body—pain free—calmed—reverent with a lightened spirit and an unburdened heart. Other drivers must have thought I was mad, smiling like a Cheshire Cat as I recalled Dinah's words. How odd and wonderful that she turned out to be a true believer of God, a loving soul connected on the astral path to the afterlife and able to give me a marvelous start on my healing process. No hocus pocus, no fortune telling.

I was excited to be home and greeted the dogs with passionate high fives.

"Hey, you guys. Guess what? We're all going to be OK."

They wagged their tails in agreement, and Thatcher went to retrieve his ball to seal the deal.

Daylight saving had arrived by this time, so although it was late in the afternoon the sun still shone brightly in the west.

I'm not waiting until tomorrow. Let's do this now.

I did as bidden and went into Megan's room and closed the door. Maybe it was my imagination taking over, I don't know, but instantly I felt Megan's presence stronger than any other time. The sun was streaming into the room, casting shadows against the opposite wall.

"Hello, Megs," softly at first. "I love you, Megan, and need your help. Together we must free Heather. She's trapped and needs me to forgive her so that she can be with you. Can I do it? Can we do it?"

I rested, closed my eyes for a moment, opened them again and looked to the window.

"Megan," I said, louder now. Her presence engulfed me, entered me, surrounded me, and was omnipotent in its power. My eyes darted around the room almost expecting to see her, the force was so great. No tears, thank God, and with tremendous strength of will I called out Heather's name.

"Heather, Heather," With increasing authority until I was shouting. "Heather! I forgive you. Heather, I forgive you. It's all right my girl, go with Megan. Free yourself of this agony. I forgive you. Take her Megs. It's OK. I want you both to be with God."

Suffer the little children to come unto Me.

A sudden moment of extreme exhaustion came over me. I looked away from the window and down to the floor.

"I forgive you, Heather," I whispered, and knew she was gone.

I sat on the end of Megan's bed and stared at my intertwined fingers, my mind a blessed blank.

Some time later my rumbling stomach reminded me of pressing mortal needs, not only for me, but for the dogs whose infinite patience with erratic feedings had to be admired. It was enough to rouse me from my state and move me to the kitchen.

There was Giles. Reality standing in the middle of the floor. I couldn't possibly tell him what I had just done, in a million years he would never understand.

"Hello, I didn't hear you come in."

"I've just got here. How are you? I thought you might like some company for supper. My secretary brought us all corncobs from her uncle's farm—too many for me on my own, and you look like you've just come home yourself. Have you thought about what you'd like to eat?"

No, I never think about food anymore. It all tastes like cardboard anyway.

"There's not much here, but I can take some chicken from the freezer and we can barbecue."

"Great. Would you like a beer?" Giles asked opening the refrigerator.

"I don't have any."

"Yeah, I see that now. OK. Well, while the chicken's defrosting I'll go to the Jiffy Store. Do you need anything else?"

"No thanks, Giles. At least I don't think so. I have salad stuff that needs eating. I'll change out of my scrubs and feed the dogs."

He was gone.

An hour ago I was excited, now I was tired and would have been glad to have the evening on my own to reflect over the last few hours. But Giles seemed to be making an effort and I suppose I should too. I wanted to talk to Ann; she would definitely understand. She would comfort me and tell me I was not losing my mind to a crackpot crystal gazer. I put in a quick call to her house but she wasn't home yet. I left a message telling her Giles was here and that I'd call again tomorrow. I knew she wouldn't call back while he was with me.

It was actually quite a pleasant evening; over supper Giles and I discussed plans for the memorial run honoring Megan, one that he had first mentioned on our trip to Atlanta. It was decided, Saturday May 10th—two weeks hence—good choice—the day before Mother's Day. Stay over I had said on impulse to Giles, and let's take the dogs to the beach on the Sunday. I was dreading Mother's day this year and knew I must make plans—stay occupied—be with family or friends—don't dwell on one of my little girls not greeting me.

I suggested the group should plant a tree in Megan's memory at the school, in the shady area next to the football stadium, and Giles reminded me of a horticulturist friend who might like to help with this. I wanted a magnolia—big and sturdy—worthy of Megan, one that would grow forever.

"Shall we plant it with some of Megan's ashes?"

"I think that would be a great idea."

It was settled; we would end the run at the house, I would prepare the food and Giles would provide a keg of beer. We thought that about fifty people might show up, old and new friends alike. I failed to tell him again that I did not want certain girls in my home, one in particular, and hoped he would remember our conversation in Atlanta. He had ever so casually mentioned that Paula would be away, and I let him off the hook by not pressing the matter further. Gail would come from Jacksonville to help me, I was sure of that, and I knew Ann, and others would also lend a hand. I offered to go to the high school to ask permission to plant the tree. I couldn't see any problem there.

The next two weeks slipped by without any dramatic incident. In spite of myself I was healing. I could go a whole minute without thinking of Megan, sometimes two. The waves of grief would come when I least expected them—walking to the parking lot on my own—oh dear God she's dead, and I would catch my breath and tremble—halt and cling to an unknown parked car for a moment before going on. Cleaning my teeth in the morning—stopping in my tracks—oh no, this can't be true, and facing my own image in the mirror, knew it was. I saw my daughter everywhere—crossing the street—pumping gas—waving her arms out of her car window. Look at this Mom, and I saw her make a nifty backward move as though her car was a tinker toy, into the only empty parking spot at the local grocery store. Our house was only a mile from her school so I heard cheer leading screams and saw daily runners, all reminders of Megan.

I wept often, silently and alone, sometimes wracking sobs of unbearable pain and other times trickles of tears left to air-dry on my cheeks. At the hospital under the weight of grief, I plodded through the day, doing only what was necessary, unable to give a scrap of extra zeal, body and spirit withered and cold. At any given opportunity between cases I would go to the hospital chapel on the first floor, kneel and pray.

'Dear God in Heaven hear my prayer. Please help me through this awful time'. Simple, but the more I prayed the more I felt sorry for myself and the more I cried. My classmates were wonderful, especially Kathy, there from the start, now shoring me up at every turn.

Helen and Gail were in daily touch with me, as was Ann. Giles called once or twice a week—short, matter-of-fact duty calls. Our relationship or future plans were never discussed.

The day of the run, Saturday, dawned bright and clear. Giles came over early, dropped his overnight bag and left to check last minute details of the actual run and to organize ice for the keg of beer. Gail drove in a little while later and I was glad of her help with the food.

"How many people are you expecting?" she asked.

"I don't really know, but at least fifty. I only hope there's enough to eat."

"Too bad," Gail said. "But by the looks of this spread, you have enough to feed an army. What time are we leaving for the run?"

An army—an army minus one.

"Three o'clock, but as you know most people will come late."

"Mom, I have a little time, would you mind if I went over to see Mandy?"

"Of course I wouldn't mind. Both she and Scott have been so good to me; I don't know what I would have done without them, especially Scott, taking so much care at Megan's funeral. Go, and remind them about this afternoon."

"So, I think I'll change into my running gear now and go straight to the school with them. See you later."

I was alone for a mere half hour before Ann showed up, followed immediately by Jane and Karen who came together. The four of us finished making sandwiches and then sat on the stoop to relax for a short while in the warmth of close friendship.

When we arrived at the High School a little after three o'clock, I was surprised to see a great number of people already gathered. Giles was there in his element, greeting many old friends and newcomers alike—a kiss here—an arm around the shoulders there and handshakes in between. It was so good to greet friends, some of whom I hadn't seen in years and had had no chance to talk to since the accident.

I was on guard however, and kept looking for the slut to show up. The later it got the more I began to relax and to think that Giles must have told her not to come after all. Wishful thinking. My heart dropped like a stone as I saw her white Honda round the corner and park under a tree.

"Look, Ann, there she is."

"Oh no. What are you going to do? No wait, you should tell your husband—let him deal with it."

"Yeah right, my husband. He won't do anything, I know him. He'll let it go—no muss, no fuss. I suppose I'll have to do it myself." And with that I marched off before anyone could stop me.

I couldn't remember the trollop's name, but no matter. She had her back to me and was tying her shoelaces against the open driver's door as I approached. Sensing rather than seeing me, she looked up.

"Look," I said in a controlled voice. "I don't care what you do on the run, but you are not welcome at my house afterwards."

That was all, no apologies, no niceties and definitely no time for her to reply as I turned tail and hastily made my way back to a very anxious looking Ann.

"What did she say?"

"Nothing. I didn't give her a chance."

Within minutes, Giles was behind me grabbing my arm, forcing me to face him.

"I hear you're up to your old tricks again," he said with such venom that I didn't immediately know what he was talking about. "You told Jodie she couldn't come back to the house and now half the group don't want to either. They want to end the run somewhere else."

Now it was my turn to be angry.

"Fine," I spat back at him. "Do what you want. I don't care anymore. But don't say I didn't warn you. I told you weeks ago I didn't want her ever coming to my house again, but you chose to ignore me. So get on with it, I don't care. Let me go." And shaking, I pulled myself free of his grip just as I could feel tears of anger starting up behind my eyes.

"Sorry, Ann. That must have been embarrassing for you to see."

Jane was nearby and also heard every word.

"I'm sorry too," she said putting a comforting arm around my shoulders. "Is there anything I can do or say?"

"Thanks, Jane. I don't think so, no. Unless you can tell me why he couldn't have stood by me for once? Especially right now."

For that, not one of us had an answer.

We watched as the group slowly began to make its way towards the football stadium to plant the tree.

Gail came running up to me.

"Are you coming, Mom? Hey-what's wrong?

"Go ahead, Gail. I'm not sure I can make it, I'm pretty upset with your father right now, but don't want to let myself down or any of our genuine friends for that matter. Go and plant the tree and I'll see you back at the house."

"Are you sure? What's Dad done this time?"

"The usual—ignoring wishes that he knows are important to me and for putting me way down on his list of priorities. I suppose I should be used to it by now, but this is a very special day and I'd hoped I would come first. I just sort of snapped. Go, Gail or you'll miss it."

"O.K. Will you be all right?"

"Sure she will," Jane interjected. "Ann and I will walk home with her."

Gail ran after the pack and quickly caught up with them.

I turned to my friends.

"Thanks guys. But you don't have to stay with me. I'll be OK."

"Nonsense. Let's go."

We walked in silence for a bit until Jane started up a conversation with Ann. Left out, I felt as though I'd been slapped in the face, but taking a breath, I realized I was glad for a moment alone.

Why was Giles so nasty? He obviously has no respect for me. Would it have killed him to honor my wishes for once?

"Would it have killed him to honor my wishes for once?" I blurted out. "Just because I refuse to be a hypocrite—just because—for once—why couldn't he stand up for me? He could think I was crazy or ill mannered or unfair, I don't care. He could have told the bitch all that and told her not to come. But no, just because he has the backbone of a bloody flea, he'd rather upset me than her. I don't understand—particularly now, why couldn't he support me? "

A steady flow of tears fell on my cheeks, tears of hurt and self-pity, anger, and despair.

Poor Ann and Jane, they had no idea what to say to me and kept silent, yet again.

"Besides, this memorial isn't just for the running group; it's for everyone who wants to honor Megan—maybe I am wrong—maybe I should have just let it go" I was ranting and knew it. "But you know, I always told my girls, stand up for yourself and your principles. Why should I tolerate someone I dislike intensely—feed her—act like I really appreciate her coming. It's not her fault, it's Giles—he should have known better—oh shit this is a nightmare."

"Maybe she won't come back," ventured Jane.

"Don't bet on it."

And I was right.

By the time we arrived back at the house the first of the runners began to appear, and a little while later the splinter group, headed by Giles and a few other die hards including Jodie surrounded the keg. They were doing their best to shield her from view. I could see her and knew what they were doing but was too busy to do anything about it at that time. I was outraged but more terribly hurt, with that gnawing sickening feeling in the pit of my stomach.

"Here, Mom, have a beer."

"I have a feeling I'm going to need more than one." I took the offered bottle from Gail.

"Stay here, Mom. I'll try talking to her—either her or Dad." Before I could say another word, Gail had moved off in the direction of the offending group gathered around the keg in the middle of the dirt road.

I should have eaten something, one beer led to another and with each one I became more and more incensed that this woman was ruining my evening, and even more incensed that I was allowing it. It was growing dark and although I lost sight of her, I could always hear her raucous laughter in the distance.

Gail reported back to me that because the keg was in the road, she wasn't officially on my property, and that if she left, the die hards—her obnoxious friends, would also leave and take the beer with them. It was all getting out of hand, with sides being taken, daggers drawn. Ann tried telling her to clear off. Jane told her in no uncertain terms she wasn't wanted, Karen appealed to any sensitivity she might have had. I even asked her politely to "please leave", all to no avail. At one point I thought she actually was going to go, but her friends circled the wagons and the nightmare continued. Giles refused to speak to me and James could only stagger about, grinning like the drunken fool he was. His girlfriend was the bitch's best ally, so he wasn't about to get involved. I had to attend to my other guests, most of whom fortunately, were unaware of the awful situation and seemed to be content enough.

The night was a total disaster. I became quite drunk and hardly said goodbye to a lot of people. I never saw Giles pick up his overnight bag and leave. I had no idea when everyone else left, what time I got to bed, or if I was alone.

I came to in a very quiet, dark house. My head was throbbing and I desperately needed water.

What time is it?

Gingerly getting out of bed, I made my way to the kitchen and saw the microwave clock: 4:25.

No! It's still the middle of the night

Siphoning water into my poor thirsty body I ventured down the passageway to the bedrooms. All were empty. Back in the sitting room I saw the glass door to the stoop had been left open and beyond, I could just make out the shapes of my two sleeping dogs. Unless there were passed out bodies in the garden, it appeared that I was indeed alone. I slumped back into bed. More sleep was impossible as I reflected on last night's events.

How could Giles have been so cruel? How could he ignore me the way he did? Why did he have total disrespect for me as his wife? I am the mother of his dead child; couldn't he have at least honored those wishes? Why the hell didn't I let it go? Why couldn't I have just turned a blind eye?

Suddenly I remembered what day it was—Sunday—Mothers Day. The first Mothers Day without Megan.

Distraction through organized mindless things—a day to be busy and mindful of Mothers Day. Pure remembrance.

And Giles and I had previously decided to take Thatcher and Liza to the beach; oh dear God, this is the part that hurts so much, alone on Mothers Day.

I cried.

I must have lain in my bed for hours, looking at the ceiling but not seeing it. The sun came up and the sky grew primrose, pink and lavender blue; still I lay there as cold and unmoving as a corpse in my coffin.

I tried not to recall the horror of the previous night. But, if I thought, rather than remembered, maybe I could avoid this new wave of pain hovering over me, about to break. If I could somehow reason it out, treat this latest tragedy as yet another hurdle to overcome, then all will be well.

I would love to think about this tomorrow.

When one of the dogs barked and jolted me back to consciousness I realized I was lying in my bed fully clothed from the night before. Slowly, I raised myself up to sit on the edge of the bed and put my hand out to turn the clock on the bedside table to face me. Nine thirty two.

I was done crying, I had nothing left. I felt sick to my stomach, ached with grief, and sagged with despair. I had two questions:

Why did Megan have to die? Why was Giles treating me this way?

My first instinct was to go to Giles, rage at him, scratch and claw, punch and kick him, do some real damage. Hadn't I suffered enough? I was filled with anger at his loathsome obsession with that damn running group of losers; that he had the gall to dismiss me as easily as flicking an annoying insect from his face. I was pacing now, fueling my anger with mortified thoughts of indignation, grinding my teeth with the realization of his insensitivity.

"SHIT!" I shouted. "Shit, oh bloody shit; shitty shitty shitty shit." And sank down on the edge of the bed shaking my head in my hands.

Well, one thing's for certain — your marriage is over.

Sod it.

I will confront Giles. I will have it out with him. I will demand an explanation.

Shower. Change. Go.

By the time I arrived at Giles's apartment I was calm but still seething. I'd had a serious talk with myself about the possible cause for his actions. I had tried intellectually reasoning about the possible outcome. Was our marriage finished?

To my chagrin Giles's truck was not in his parking space.

Damn. I got myself all worked up for nothing. Yes, but you're secretly relieved aren't you. Your heart rate is racing with the prospect of confrontation. Slow down. Think.

I sat in my car wondering what to do.

I had a key; should I go in anyway? Maybe someone else brought him home?

I looked around to see if I recognized any other car in the parking lot.

To hell with this. What do you care if he's inside his apartment or not? Or if he's alone. Don't be a coward. Do it.

I walked up the stairs and knocked on his door. I knocked again, this time harder. Nothing. *OK here we go.* Inside the front door I called out.

"Giles, are you home? Is anyone here?"

All was quiet. With trepidation I crept toward his bedroom. Empty. The bed was unmade, the whole room an untidy mess, but something told me Giles had not come home last night. I resumed normal breathing and went into Megan's room. It was then I started to cry. Again. Only a few of her things were there, but all were significant—the swimming trophies won at State—photos of her friends on and off the swim team—a stereo, her favorite teddy bear sleeping on the neatly made bed, drawers stuffed with swimsuits and clothes hanging in the closet. I thought about the decision we'd made for Megan to have a room in both houses—my need for space when things got rough between us. Those fights are small and insignificant now aren't they?

"Megan, it's Mothers Day, and you know don't you," I cried out loud. "You know all about your father."

Fanned by woe and bitter resentment, anger was building up in me again—puffs of wind over dying embers.

You bastard, where are you?

I fiercely wiped the tears from my face and decided to take everything of Megan's back to my house. Driven by a passionate fury, I gathered up armfuls of clothes still on hangers and descended the outside stairs to my car. I found plastic garbage bags and piled in stuff from shelves and drawers all mixed up together. I took photographs from the refrigerator doors, toothbrushes from the bathroom, even the sheets off the bed. Trip after trip, up and down the stairs until not one vestige of Megan remained in the apartment. On the last descent I bumped into Giles's downstairs neighbor, a pleasant, older woman I'd met only once before, but by all accounts from Megan, one that had been very good to her.

"Hello. Happy Mothers Day."

"Yeah. Right."

"Where's Giles? Is he home?"

"No, and I don't know or care where he is." And I rudely pushed past her to my car. Once behind the driving wheel, I exploded in tears of bottled up anger, but rapidly drove away so as not to embarrass her or myself further.

I knew I had to calm down, but I didn't want to go home and wallow in the misery of self-sorrow. I stopped at the first road sign, dried my eyes and blew my nose. It was a special day and most people would be celebrating with family, especially their Moms. Ann was on the west coast with hers, Karen and Jane at home with theirs. I was the only one of our little group of friends who didn't have a mother, at least not in the flesh.

Mum, help me please.

I needed to be in public somewhere and decided to go to the steak restaurant where Megan, Gail and I had all been servers. At 2pm it was crowded, as I knew it would be today, but Rebecca, my manager of old was delighted to see me and squeezed me into a spot at the bar. I filled her in with brief details of the night before and eventually said out loud.

"Rebecca, I think this is the end of my marriage."

She wisely said not a word but grasped both of my hands and nodded her agreement.

"I'm going to get you something to eat and I won't take no for an answer," she informed me, departing for the kitchen. From my position at the bar I looked around and recognized a couple of familiar faces of regular customers, but I was not in the mood to make polite conversation with anyone, I kept my head down and slowly drank the beer Rebecca had served me. I was tired. More, I was sick and tired of feeling horribly distressed, tired of feeling dejected, rejected, bodily sick of the sham. It was pitiful I should feel so betrayed, so unimportant—inconsequential—*whoops, don't go crying again, no pity party here.*

Fortunately, just in the nick of time, a plate of food was delivered, a scrumptious filet mignon accompanied by a hot steaming baked potato.

Oh, Rebecca, you could not have done a nicer thing for me today.

Chapter Twenty

It was two weeks before I saw Giles again. Neither of us had attempted contact; He'd hurt me so badly, I would have gone to my grave never speaking to him again. In a dreamlike state I managed to get through those days powered by adrenalin, often immobilized by huge waves of grief, mixed grief, for Megan, for my seemingly doomed marriage and for the empty mess I had become. I was like a mechanical doll, existing by rote. There were large gaps of missing time and on return to reality, I wondered what I should have been doing. Some days were punctuated by sharp reminders of that detestable event, the evening of humiliation when my husband had abandoned me. In vain I desperately tried to ignore them. At night it wasn't as easy as I tossed and turned in my bed, slivers of memories invading my brain from every angle preventing any worthwhile sleep. During the day I was forced to concentrate on school with final exams looming in less than a week. I'd come so far, I must not fail. I only spoke to Ann and Jane about the injustice of that awful night, and they couldn't begin to understand Giles' behavior, but passed it off as peer pressure or booze talk or his way of dealing with grief. Although I knew they supported me, I got the impression they didn't want to hear about it anymore.

Whatever.

The next Saturday morning I was giving Thatcher a bath out on the grass when I glanced up to see Giles striding towards me.

Well, I do declare.

"Would you like a hand with that?" he nonchalantly asked.

"Sure, I've nearly finished, but if you'd like to bring me the towel I left on the stoop, that would help."

My heart was beating fast, my mind confused. Jane had reported to me that Giles and Paula had been spotted huddled together in a downtown bar, and as soon as they realized they'd been seen, had left immediately. I wasn't surprised, but I was surprised at how much Giles could still hurt me.

What does he want? Is he here to make amends? Or is he going to tell me it's all over? Stay calm.

Together we finished the slippery process of initially drying Thatcher before he could run back into the house and shake, a game I knew he loved to play.

"He's such a good swimmer and loves to be in water, I can't understand why he doesn't like to be bathed." Giles rubbed his hands on the edge of the towel.

We released the still wet dog to race around the yard and watched him roll over and over in the grass, his way of drying the inside of his ears.

"Would you like a cup of tea?"

"Great, thanks."

I picked up the dog shampoo before we walked into the house and I made sure I busied myself with the simple task of making tea. I was nervous—suddenly unsure of myself—lacking confidence—but. . .

I am not going to ask him how he is. I'm not going to mention his absence of late, and I'm definitely not going to bring up that dreadful night.

After a very long silence when the awkwardness between us had to be broken, I said.

"I'm graduating next Thursday. I don't suppose you would like to come? Gail is coming down, and Ann and Jane. You don't have to ..."

"Yes, Gail told me about it. Sure, I'll be there."

So that's why he's here. He's got a guilty conscience. I bet Gail told him he had to come. It wouldn't look good if he missed the ceremony, and he couldn't turn up on the night without seeing me beforehand. Bloody hell, Giles, now I can see through you like a pane of glass.

"I don't want to go, but it's mandatory, and I've got to wear that awful silky gown and stupid hat with a stupid tassel," I snorted. "I'm sure I'll be the oldest one there like some geriatric wannabe."

"Nonsense," said Giles. "Age doesn't matter and you should be very proud of yourself. It must have been very hard for you to go back to school when you did."

Head down, he fidgeted with the spoon in the saucer of his teacup and was obviously uncomfortable, but I wasn't about to make him feel any better. I was empty inside, done, devoid of feeling. No, not really, but I had no idea what I felt for Giles. Certainly at this moment I had nothing to give him, and even less inclination to make an effort to do so.

The empty space between us was becoming wider and wider, until eventually Giles said, "Well, I've got to be off now. Let me know where to go and the time and I'll see you there."

"OK. Maybe we could all go out for a drink afterwards."

"We'll see."

There was no bodily contact from either of us and a minute later I watched him drive away.

Damn.

Why ask him that? It's obvious he's only coming out of duty and doesn't want to socialize.

It didn't take you long to get back on the eggshell path did it?

Graduation Day. And I'd never felt so foolish in my whole life—all dressed up in a silly costume, and about as enthusiastic as a prisoner awaiting the gallows. But I dutifully smiled for the group photo and tried to join in with the hugs and best wishes from my classmates. My school friend Kathy sat beside me, miserable that her mother who had died six months previously, would not be there to see her graduate.

Your mother, Kathy, and my daughter. I wonder if the angels could arrange for them to be together to watch us.

With over two hundred people from all the different classes gathered in the assembly hall, it was a long boring ceremony, speech after speech from every faculty member and then some. My thoughts drifted to Megan, just three months shy of graduating high school—what a shame—with a full scholarship to college waiting for her—such a bright future…When my turn eventually came to walk across the stage to receive my certificate from the dean, and my name was announced, all I could hear was a whoop and whistle from Jane, Ann and Gail at the back of the hall.

God Almighty, hold it down.

But I turned to grin at them, raised the blank rolled up piece of paper tied with red ribbon, a graduate's bogus certificate, above my head in the traditional triumphant salute of degree.

It was better, afterwards, outside. The air had cooled after a slight rain shower. The flash of camera bulbs, noisy groups of laughing, happy people slowly dispersing into the night. I met up with my family and friends—kisses and words of congratulations, although no kiss from Giles. He was somewhat stiff, but honorably bound to do the right thing.

"Let's all go to the pub," said Jane linking her arm through mine and steering me towards the parking lot.

"I'll meet you there," said Ann. "I'm parked at the corner."

"Me too," echoed Gail. "Mom, I'll come for a while but I have to get back to Jacksonville tonight. I have a big exam coming up in two days and need to study some more." She put her arm around me and kissed my cheek. "I'm so proud of you and Megan would have been too. I'm sure Helen called you didn't she? Congratulations, you did it."

"Thanks. And thanks for coming down, Gail."

Giles lingered behind us.

"What about you, Giles," I asked him over my shoulder. "Are you coming?"

"No, I think I'll be going. You go and enjoy yourselves."

It was as though he'd punched me in the stomach, I could have vomited on his boots.

You rotten, rotten bastard. Can't you spare me one celebratory drink? You're probably going off to meet Paula aren't you? Put in your dues and thankful it's all over. Oh how I hate you. You bloody rotten bastard.

I couldn't look at him and forced myself not to cry.

"Bye." I said as curtly as I could muster and I'd be damned if I was going to thank him for coming. Turning my back on him I walked away with Gail and Jane to my car.

It took all my strength of will that night to sit in the pub and pretend to be happy. The chicken sandwich stuck in my throat like cotton wool, and the beer felt like lumpy gravy, but I didn't want to spoil the mood of my friends, they were so happy for me. I was devastated Giles didn't want to be there and the gnawing sick feeling in my gut remained well after I'd left the pub and returned home alone, all hope sucked out of me, depressed beyond reason. Thank God for the dogs and my beloved cat, Roger,—cold noses and a purr—saviors that kept me from going completely under.

Friday, our last day of school. We did nothing but receive our real graduation certificates, talk about the highs and lows of the past year and wish one another good luck in the future. I was home by eleven.

Still angry and hurt at Giles for not coming to the pub, I decided he must pay the mortgage on the house a bit longer. I was in no fit state to cope with big decisions like selling a house and moving, (to where?) and (with whom?) so I called the realtor and told her to come and pick up her "For Sale" sign. Another six months wouldn't hurt anyone. Besides I needed more time; I hadn't yet gone into Megan's room to pack up her stuff. All her things I'd brought from Giles's apartment on Mothers Day remained on her bed where I'd dumped them. I needed to psyche myself up to tackle that, but I sensed I would know when the time was right. I also knew Megan would help me.

I started my new job the following Monday, and quite by coincidence, one of my fellow workers was also a swim mother, and old friend. Her daughter, although attending a different High school, had been a laughing archrival of Megan's and the pair alternated wins at the various meets over the years. It was great to see Ginny, and a wonderful comfort to have her in the operating room with me not only as a mentor, guiding me professionally in a strange new place, but also as a warm understanding person, saying little but knowing everything. She definitely helped me through the first few weeks, and often during our breaks together we would talk about Megan, and swimming and the paralleled life we both had shared. It was impossible not to well up with tears, or even cry a little, but everyone at my new place of work was wonderful, so that hour by hour, day by day I slowly continued to heal.

Within a couple of weeks I discovered another nurse, Jo, owned a female springer spaniel named Abby, who was due to come into heat any day. Abby was black and white whereas Thatcher was brown and white. That didn't matter—the prospect of tri-colored puppies really excited us, especially Thatcher. We arranged for him to pay his respects and when the appropriate time came, a love match was declared when he spent the weekend at Jo's house, never leaving Abby for a minute. All we had to do now was wait.

Meanwhile, Giles had resumed his weekend visits when we walked both dogs on country trails. He usually stayed for lunch and was gone shortly thereafter. Sometimes we would go to the cinema or for a bike ride in the evening, but the occasions were flat, with no discussions about the future. Why he came I'll never know, because we only made small talk, never brought up the infamous "night of shame", never spoke of anybody at the running group, and worse, hardly mentioned Megan's name.

One night we were walking down the lane, giving Thatcher and Liza their last walk before bed, the last before he went back to his apartment. I hated that. I hated being left alone. I felt like a misused mistress when sex had gone bad, only in this case there was no sex, not a hint of it—no bloody physical contact at all. I casually put my hand in his. It was tolerated for about six seconds and then he shook me free. I couldn't believe it—he actually shook me off. My patience was at an end.

"For God's sake, Giles, you've got to try," I yelled. "If we're going to have any life together you've got to make an effort. Otherwise we might just as well be divorced."

"Is that what you want?"

'No," I cried. "But we can't go on like this. It's ridiculous."

"What do you want to do?"

"I want resolution. No, I don't want a divorce. I want to try to put things back together. I'm even willing to go to a counselor."

"Well, I think our marriage as it was is over. We can't go back, but I fail to see how paying a complete stranger ninety dollars an hour to fix our problems will help. I'm not about to do that. You can go on your own if you like."

"Giles." I was so exasperated. He always avoided confrontation especially on this issue, and now, when we finally were discussing our future, he was so negative. But I battled on.

"You—we—we must make an effort. I'm not prepared to give up. We've been married twenty-five years; surely that means something to you?" And when he didn't reply, I softly said more to myself than him, "maybe not."

We had returned to his truck.

"It's late, we'll talk about this another time. See you next week. Goodnight."

He was gone and I was left in the driveway more in despair than at any other time.

Bloody hell. Giles—oh bloody hell.

A week went by with only one phone call from Giles. He would come to the house Sunday not Saturday as originally planned as there was a big July fourth run planned for the Saturday. I could go with him if I liked.

Are you crazy? Never in a million years.

Fine, it didn't matter to me one day or another, each one slipped by without much effort from me. I went to work, came home, ate dinner, and went to bed. No plans, no interest, no energy.

I was up early that Sunday morning, around seven, made my tea and went out on the verandah to look for the dogs outside. I could see Thatcher lying under the big cypress tree, and Liza not far off. She heard me and came lopping over to push her way through the doggy flap of the wire netted porch.

"Hello my girl," I said to her while rubbing her ears. "Are you ready for your long walk today? Come, Thatcher." I called to him, but he didn't stir. My heart skipped a beat as I opened the porch door and made my way to the tree. Still he didn't move.

"Thatcher? Oh no, please no."

As I approached I looked to see if he was breathing. "Oh no, no, no." Until finally I stood beside him and his glassed over eyes stared back at me. Slowly I knelt down to touch his cold stiff body. "Oh, no. Oh Thatcher, what happened to you?"

There wasn't a mark on him, no blood, no wounds, and no signs of being bitten or beaten up. I looked at him for the longest while trying to make sense of it. Tears welled in my eyes, but did not overflow.

"You poor little bugger," I said out loud. I didn't move him but went back inside and sat looking out over the rose garden until Giles arrived an hour later.

"Thatcher's dead." I told him in a flat voice.

"What—how—." Giles was obviously stunned. "Why didn't you call me?"

"I don't know. You're here now."

"Where is he?"

I got out of my chair and led him to the tree. It was only then I cried a slow trickle of tears as I watched Giles turn over the body of my much loved dog and examine him for any reason for death.

"What do you think happened?" he asked me.

"I don't know, but I think a car must have hit him and he had just enough strength to crawl back to this tree."

"How a car could hit him and not stop," moaned Giles. "That's beyond me."

"Well, maybe the car killed him outright and the driver brought him here, the dogs are well known in this neighborhood; but if that happened I would have thought there would be a bloody wound somewhere. I didn't hear anything either and I think he's been dead for sometime." I turned away, unable to look at him any longer. "He could have had a heart attack or stroke, but he's only eighteen months old, so I don't think that's plausible. Maybe a coral snake bit him. They're deadly. Unless we have an autopsy we'll never know for sure."

"You don't want to do that do you?" Giles asked. "I'm sure that would be very expensive, and what if it proved to be inconclusive… "his sentence trailed off.

I saw Giles shake his head from side to side. "What a shame! He was a good dog. We'd better bury him alongside Molly." (our springer spaniel we'd brought from Costa Rica who'd died two years ago at the age of twelve (old age for a springer))

It had started to rain and so it was a pitiful burial ceremony at the bottom of the garden with Liza and Roger looking on. I swear they both knew.

"What do you want to do today? Do you want to walk with just Liza? Not much fun without Thatcher and I think this rain will last all day."

"I don't know. Nothing." I was very sad, all choked up but with no real tears. A good wholesome cry might help, but the tears I needed for release wouldn't come. All I wanted to do was curl up and die too; my lovely, beloved, wonderful dog who'd given me so much joy, so much comfort, was gone.

I love you Thatcher. Go to Megan. She'll take care of you.

"We need to get out," declared Giles. "We mustn't sit around here all day. Let's go to the Science Museum, I believe there's a new exhibition just started, and we'll be indoors out of the rain."

"Whatever—I don't care." I bent to give Liza a hug. "You're going to miss him, Liza, aren't you, probably more than any of us."

I felt as heavy as lead as I went to change clothes, with those same sickening feelings of grief, my eyes constantly filled with tears. I didn't believe I could love a dog as much as I loved Thatcher.

God, what are You doing? Why are you taking everything I've ever loved away from me? What have I done to piss You off? Something from my past? I swear I meant to pay for the stolen candy when I was six. What's next? I was always taught to love and trust You without question, but this isn't fair. Megan's with Molly, she doesn't need Thatcher. Why, why why?

It seemed the whole world and his wife and kids were at the Science Museum that Sunday afternoon which was just as well for me. My heart wasn't in it, but there was enough distraction to prevent me from bawling in public. Giles was nice to me, encouraged me to eat something, and did his best to cheer me up, but I was not easily consoled.

Thatcher.

It was a morose journey back along the interstate. Slumped in the passenger seat of Giles's truck, I was feeling very sorry for myself, frowning with unhappiness and racked with pain over the loss of my daughter, my dog, probably my marriage and the way of life, as I'd known it. To my surprise I suddenly blurted out.

"Are you having an affair with Paula?"

"No."

"Have you ever had an affair with her?"

"No."

"Well, I've been told you were seen together in a downtown bar."

"Yeah, I knew that would get back to you. She's a good friend of mine, that's all."

"Quite honestly, Giles, I don't believe you. Every time I've seen you together, you've been mighty chummy. Whether you're having an affair with her or not, she has not shown me any respect. Neither of you have. Do you really think I needed to see you two huddled like lovers while I'm still mourning the loss of Megan? You are still my husband."

"You can believe what you want, but I'm telling you there's nothing going on. Paula's had tragedy in her life too."

"Not right now she hasn't." The pitch of my voice rising. "She's never been married or lost a child. What makes her need greater than mine?"

He didn't reply, and we drove the rest of the way home in silence.

At the house Giles did not turn off the engine of his truck. He turned to me and asked.

"Would you like me to stay with you this evening?"

"No, I don't think so, there's no point."

"OK then—you sure you'll be all right." It was so obvious he was desperate to leave.

"I'll be fine," I said opening my door and taking out the keys to the house.

"See you next week. Call me if you need anything."

Yeah, right. Let me tell you, Giles, the way I'm feeling right now, you'd be the last person I'd call.

It was horrible entering the house without Thatcher; so quiet, so empty. I made a huge fuss over Liza who nuzzled her face into my lap and wouldn't leave my side.

"Where are you Rog?" Looking around and not seeing my cat. "Let's find him, Liza."

We found him in his usual spot, curled up in the middle of my bed. He raised his head and mewed his greeting. I loved that cat, I loved the way he talked to me, and I loved the comfort he gave me. He was there now in my hour of need and I mewed back a "hello", but didn't disturb him.

I called Ann. I had to tell her the news about Thatcher and I knew she would be devastated along with me. And she was.

"That's not the worst of it, Ann," I went on. "Giles and I went to the Science Museum today, which was good; I knew we mustn't mope around here all day. Although it was a sad day for both of us, everything was reasonably fine until we were driving home and I confronted him about Paula. Honestly, Ann, the words were out of my mouth before I realized what I was saying."

"Oh my God, how did he answer you?"

"Well, it was more of what he didn't say really. Of course he denied having an affair with her—"we're just good friends"—"I enjoy talking to her"—"she's had tragedy in her life" bla, bla, bla. But then when I asked him how her need was greater than mine, he clammed up and we drove the rest of the way home without another word."

"Good for you," said Ann. "At least you had the courage to finally ask him about her."

"I also told him that I thought neither of them have any respect for me in my grief for Megan."

"That's true," said Ann agreeing with me. "He's not there now with you is he?"

"No way. It sickens me to even look at him. Tell me something, why do I continue to push on trying to save my marriage, when in my heart I know it's all over."

"Because you took sacred vows that are very important to you."

"Yeah right, for better or for worse, but it seems Giles is only a fairweather husband. Those vows obviously don't mean much to him."

"I know he's done you wrong, and I'm the last one to defend him," went on Ann. "But give him a bit longer. You never know down the road, what's going to happen? I don't think he can cope with Megan's loss as well as you."

"Maybe you're right," I conceded. "He's always held his emotions in check, enough that I sometimes wonder if he has any at all. I'll confess to you, Ann, I never saw him shed a tear over Megan, or break down in any way. For his sake I hope he did so in private. He prides himself on being a great communicator but in truth our communication skills are abysmal. If our marriage is over, why doesn't he come right out and tell me?"

"Well, that's obvious," said Ann. "He knows you can't take any more grief at this time."

"It would be better than this thread hanging," I replied.

"No, I don't think so," said Ann, for the first time disagreeing with me. "You are still in deep mourning for your daughter—and now Thatcher. I don't think you realize how fragile you are, you can't take any more, and Giles knows you well enough to realize it. You have yet another hurdle to overcome this week with Megan's birthday coming up—it's too much."

"We didn't even discuss that. He's so awful at remembering anyone's birthday, even his own, that he probably doesn't realize it's hers on Wednesday. It hurts me though, Ann, that he hardly mentions her name. It's as though it's all over, done and dealt with, nothing you can do about it attitude, no point in grieving any more, let's go forward. He was the same when my mother died—too bad—cry for a day now get over it."

"Men and women are so different," said Ann still in Giles's defense. "That's why girlfriends are so important. So, are we still on for Wednesday?"

"Sure, I'm looking forward to it and dreading it, all at the same time."

"We'll have a good day I promise. Kenny's calling me—I'd better go. See you next week and take care."

"Thanks, Ann. 'Bye."

I put the phone down and thought about what I had just said. It was going to be Megan's nineteenth birthday on Wednesday and because it was a weekday and would be quiet, Ann had thoughtfully arranged for the two of us to spend the day at a National Park just north of Orlando and take a boat trip up the St John's River to look for 'gators. That would be nice, but without Megan?

Megs, my darling, please arrange your schedule to be with us then.

Was it my imagination that I thought I could hear her laugh?

Come to me.

I closed my eyes and summoned all my concentration to see Megan—laughing—dancing—sprawled in a chair—talking on the phone—eating French fries—goofing off—the list went on, the images as vivid as truth, a virtual kaleidoscope of memorabilia redeemed from oblivion. I gave in to the slide show, slumped in an armchair, unable to move a muscle. When Megan's turn finished, Thatcher came into view, swimming in his favorite lake, swimming for the sheer joy of it, grinning as he climbed the bank to shake himself free of excess water. Megan and Thatcher playing in a friend's pool—a toss up who was having the most fun.

I don't know how long I sat there alone in the dark wrapped in an invisible cloak of nothingness, until with a jolt Giles and Paula disturbed my peace. What was I going to do about that? I didn't have enough energy to even adjust my feelings and moved only enough to get to bed without supper. I couldn't be bothered.

Chapter Twenty - One

It was tough at work the next day. We were a small group, and everyone was so sad to hear about Thatcher, especially Jo. But she was almost sure her bitch, Abby, was pregnant, and wouldn't that be a wonderful lasting legacy for my dog.

As with the previous night, alternate images of Megan and Thatcher kept flashing before me and for most of the morning I was either welling up with tears or overflowing with them. I couldn't concentrate for any length of time, so that by lunchtime I was sent home. I don't know whether that was a good or bad thing. My compassionate nursing supervisor obviously saved me more embarrassment at work, but when I arrived home I faced the ghastly quiet of an empty house, a hollowness dooming me to calamitous thoughts.

Indeed, I moped around all afternoon, cried some more, didn't eat, didn't check messages, didn't bring in the mail, ignored all telephone calls and finally dozed off while watching some inane soap opera on TV.

Did you know I'm going to be ten tomorrow, Mom?

No, really, Megan?

You did.

No, honestly love, if I'd known I would have bought you a present.

Mom!
No, really—no really—no really…

I suddenly came to, with pain shooting over my right shoulder from a crick in my neck. That's all I need I thought as I raised myself sideways out of the chair and gingerly stretched.

There's pain involved with everything I do or say or think these days.

I was still trying to come to terms with the way I felt about Giles. One moment I was ashamed of my bitterness towards him, seemingly unable to stop myself, and the next frustrated at his inability to soothe me. Did I still love him? Good question. I would dearly love to call him right now, tell him I've had a rotten day and to come over just to put his arms around me. I shook my head from side to side knowing that was never going to happen.

Instead I turned to my daughters and called one after the other. Both were extremely upset yesterday when I told them of Thatcher's death, and both were glad to hear from me now although I wasn't in a much better frame of mind.

"Things will get better, Mom," Helen told me. "Hang in there. I wish I was living closer to be of greater help to you, but I'd like you to consider coming up to Chicago to visit me. It would do you good to get away for a bit. Eric's coming for a long weekend at the end of August, how about you come too?"

"Surely you don't want me there then."

"Why not? It'll be fun, and the three of us can explore Chicago together."

"Thanks, darling. I will think about it."

Helen could not ignore my huge sigh and continued.

"Mom, I know Wednesday is going to be very difficult, but you'll be with Ann, and you know I'll be constantly thinking of you. Is there anything else I can do?"

"Thanks, but no," I was holding back tears. "I'll be all right. I'll let you go now. I love you."

"I love you too. I'm here if you need me. Bye."

The call to Gail was much the same, and of course I was comforted by their words, but the minute they hung up the phone I went into a dead slump again. The silence was unbearable, the effort to breathe, draining. I was careening backwards and knew I was out of control, unable and not willing to fix it. I missed Megan so *much* I was going insane, with great chunks of time tossed off to indifference. Even the most mundane of tasks became a huge chore and often went undone. I hated myself for feeling so bitter. I loathed the "woe is me" attitude. I had to pull myself together, but how?

I took Liza for a walk up the dirt road. Somehow being outside in the fresh air both revived me a little and had a calming effect. Megan wouldn't want to see me like this. I would be no use to anyone including myself if I continued to break down. Megan's gone. Thatcher's gone. You can't do anything about either of them. You must go on—stay strong—be the capable person you know you are. Relax a little—let events take their course—leave Giles alone— don't try to fix everything at once. You're getting too far ahead of yourself. Remember all the advice given to you by well-meaning mourners—stay busy—take one day at a time—call on friends to help...

OK. Enough already.

I turned for home. My own advice lasted a very short while. I drank a couple of beers, nibbled at some potato chips, fed Liza and Roger, watched some easily forgotten television and went to bed as devastated as I'd been the first week after Megan's death.

I did not sleep.

Tuesday morning I called in sick. I knew it was the wrong thing to do but I was past caring—*stay busy—don't be alone. Go away, I want to wallow.*

I did not dress, nor did I shower and spent most of the morning sitting in my favorite rocking chair on the stoop staring into space like some catatonic schizophrenic. I forced myself to eat a boiled egg for lunch, crawled back into bed and fell into the ever- deepening black morass of despair. It was bad.

Miracles of miracles. Don't ask how but I awoke with a lightened heart.

Happy birthday, Megan. Happy birthday, my girl.

The giant mallet that had been hammering me down, down, down into that pit of depression had been lifted. No longer feeling paralyzed by grief, I could breathe, and see without the veil of tears. Although it wasn't exactly with a joyous spirit that I prepared for the day on the river with Ann, I couldn't help but smile as I remembered Megan's birth, the easiest and quickest of the three. She looked so like her sister, Helen when she was born, that even Giles remarked on the similarity. Immediately following her birth, Megan and I had been separated for a short nap, and in what seemed like the next moment, his new daughter in his arms, Giles had brought her to me.

"I've got someone here who wants her Mummy," he had said.

I looked down to this incredible child—so perfect—so beautiful, big brown eyes open wide and alert, unaffected it seemed by the effort to be born. Here in my arms was love. She was mine. I feasted my eyes on this precious scrap, taking in every pore, examining every angel's breath of hair. A sudden thought

"You're not Sarah," I said, remembering the name we'd previously picked. "Giles, I'd like to call her Megan. Is that all right with you?"

"Fine by me."

Megs, you were such a good baby.

The day was bearable. Looking for 'gators wouldn't have been my first choice of things to do; they are such ugly creatures not known for their felicitous abilities. Then again they always appeared to have smiles on their faces, so if it works for them—but the sun, the river, the birds, the company of a few other people in a boat gently cruising on the water, was in fact, the best medicine. Ann, bless her heart, was a superb comforter with or without words. Over lunch she asked about Megan's birthdays with genuine interest, and it was so great to talk about my daughter knowing I wasn't boring anyone. Once I got started, I warmed to the theme and recounted many happy birthdays, especially the last eighteenth one when her father and I presented her with a new car, the little green Toyota Corolla. She'd been overjoyed to the point of hysteria, and took off in a flash to show it to all her friends.

Drive carefully...

I was back on track thankful that another emotional day was over. Having been warned that any significant occurrence like a birthday, throughout the first year following a tragedy, would be disturbing, I was surprised that Megan's actual birthday wasn't nearly as bad as the days leading up to it. I was always better dealing with reality rather than dreadful speculation, and just lately, especially after Thatcher's death, it seemed every new day was a reinvention of me, and I never could guess as to how I might be.

I settled into a routine at work and Giles resumed sporadic visits at the weekends. I heeded my own advice—went with the flow, especially with him. We didn't have much in common any more, but I was past caring. I never brought up the future and never discussed the past. If he couldn't meet me half way, why should I try for the both of us? The one thing I wanted to talk about but couldn't summons the courage for was what to do with Megan's ashes. Giles had them at his apartment, which was fine by me for the moment, but I didn't want him to have them all forever. Some were already planted with the magnolia tree at the high school—the rest—not sure, but I did have stirrings of a plan to scatter them over the stones of Stonehenge in my native city of Salisbury in England. Megan had fallen in love with the place on a visit there when she was fifteen, and as it is my wish for my ashes, what better than to have Megan waiting there for me.

The good news was that Jo's dog, Abby was indeed pregnant. *Thatcher you should be so proud.*
On August 19th I got a phone call from Jo at six in the morning.
"She's started."
"Oh, yes! That's great. I'll be right over."
Good for you, Abby. How considerate of you to have your babies on a Saturday morning. By the time I got to Jo's house two puppies had been cleaned up and were seemingly abandoned to one side of the crate.
"She's about to have another," said Jo, and sure enough out popped one more. All three so far were liver and white males. By the middle of the afternoon, Abby had given birth to nine pups, five females, four males and three of them tri-colored.
"They're beautiful," I said. "And I know I'm going to have a tough job picking one."
On the way home I pondered which puppy I should choose— male or female? —Or whether I ought to have another dog at all, but then seeing Liza all alone in the back yard, I knew at least one decision was made.
My oldest daughter's persuasive abilities proved to be very

powerful, so at the end of August I went up for the long Labor Day weekend in Chicago with Helen and Eric. It was great. I loved the city and delighted in playing tourist visiting all the renowned spots. One night we took a boat trip on Lake Michigan to look back on the lit up shore line, and another we were thoroughly entertained on the Gangsters bus tour with "mob driver Al Capone" pointing out the spots of all his notorious victories. It was good to laugh, it was good to feel comfortable with family (by now I considered Eric part of ours) and it was good not to be totally consumed by wretched misery.

Late Sunday night when we'd just gone to bed, but weren't yet asleep, the phone rang.

Helen answered and I heard her say 'Oh no'

I hated middle of the night calls and lay still in my bed, heart already thumping, not daring to breathe. Light streamed in through my open door as Helen handed me the phone.

"It's Gail."

"Mom, sorry to call you so late—did Helen tell you? I've just heard—Princess Diana was killed in a road crash today. Isn't that awful?"

"Oh my God. Yes, terrible. What happened?"

"There're very few details yet. She was in Paris with her boyfriend and they'd left a restaurant—I don't know any more, and obviously it's all over the news now. I didn't mean to wake you, but thought you'd like to know."

"Yes, thanks. And no, I wasn't asleep. What a shame. Dear oh dear, she was so lovely." I looked at Helen. "Turn on the TV. Yes, Gail. Right. It's on here as well. Oh my God, this is too awful." We watched in silence for a bit. "Well, we could sit up all night and watch this, but there's not much more to say now is there? We'd better get back to bed. I'll call you tomorrow."

"OK. Sorry, Mom. I didn't mean to spoil your trip, and I hope you're having a good time with Helen and Eric?"

"Yes, a great time. I love Chicago. I'll call you tomorrow and tell you more. Thanks for calling, Gail. I love you."

"Love you too. Bye."

There wasn't much more to say to Helen and Eric and no point in staying up. I couldn't bear to see Diana's mangled car one more time; it only served as a grim reminder of a little green Toyota Corolla. As I closed my eyes to try to sleep, all I could think of was how sorry I felt for Diana's Mum. I understood her agony perfectly.

Back in Florida on Saturday the ninth of September I rose early, made my tea and turned on the TV. to watch Princess Diana's funeral. One hour later, in tears, I called Giles.

"It's so sad," I told him. "Please come over and watch it with me."

"I would," he replied. "But I've arranged to meet James and a few others for an early morning run."

Instantly I could feel anger rising up within my soul. Dammit, why couldn't he meet my wishes just once? I needed him. Why did I always come last on his list of priorities? But, as so often in the past I deferred with silent resignation.

Don't make a fuss.

"I'll come over later," I heard Giles say. "You'll be OK."

"All right. 'Bye."

Now I was really irate. How dare he tell me I was OK when I was anything but? But my animosity slowly surrendered to despair as I resumed watching the television and joined my fellow Brits and the entire world in their sorrow over losing a cherished princess.

Later, having decided I didn't want to see or speak to Giles or anyone else. I went to the mall, not to buy anything in particular, but knowing I couldn't trust myself not to fall into a huge pit of depression by being alone. It worked for a short while, but then I found myself wandering absolutely aimlessly, as though my eyes were closed, not bothering to even look into the shop windows, or caring to avoid oncoming traffic. What I thought would ward off depression was in fact making me worse. Alone in my marriage, alone in a crowd. With enormous effort I made my way to the food court. Once there, I realized I was starving and wanted French fries, which I ate without a shred of guilt.

Once in a while won't kill you.

But the out of control children, screaming parents, and noisy half clad teenagers grated on my nerves, further sending me into melancholia, and forcing me to leave. Where to go?

I turned my car towards home and on the way stopped at the high school. There was no game, no activity at all, the parking lot was empty but the gates were still open. I pulled up beside the football field, stood by the fence and looked over to the magnolia tree newly planted in Megan's honor, now gently swaying in the breeze. I stared at the plaque staked at the foot that denoted her name and the one word simple inscription "Champion".

Yes, you were my girl. Indeed, you were always my champion right from your first breath. I love you Megan. I love you. Have you any idea how much I miss you?

For the longest time I gazed at the fifteen foot sapling that would grow with Megan's spirit into a fine tall tree.

"I hope you live for ever," I said out loud, and reluctantly walked back to my car.

There were messages on my answering machine from Helen, Gail, both my brothers in England and Ann, but nothing from Giles. I hoped he'd been to the house and left when I wasn't there. I did not want to see him. I did not want to see anyone, and had no intention of returning telephone calls.

This day was the beginning of a downward spiral into a depressive state like I'd never experienced. I was so dejected that I couldn't to do anything but mope about without cause. The mere effort of existing was enough. I had never felt so alone in my life—desolate—comfortless, which in turn created a weariness that led to more heartache as I floundered to survive. I felt I had a broken brain and was spinning on a terrifying self-induced wheel of misery. How to stop? I had no idea, and less energy to care.

The black embrace of loneliness stayed with me for the rest of the weekend, during which time I received many more phone calls, all of which remained unanswered and unreturned. Late Sunday afternoon, unannounced, I looked up from my chair to find Ann standing over me. Just like that. No car noises, no side door opening. She materialized.

"I've been so worried about you. Are you all right? I thought there might be something wrong with your phone as you haven't answered my calls?"

"I'm fine. I didn't feel like talking to anyone and would like to be left alone."

"Look," Ann pressed on. "I know you're depressed and you have every right to be. You've been through so much—Lord knows where you got the strength—but please let me help you now."

"I don't need help. Go away."

Ann was so shocked by my curt tone that she took a step back.

"OK." she said. "I'll go. But you do need help. We're all worried about you—you don't have to go through this alone—there are so many willing people and if you won't let me do it, then please—go to somebody else, but promise me you won't do anything stupid. I care about you so much, and your daughters love you, and your animals need you, and—please, if you change your mind, I beg you to call me any time of the day or night; I'll drop everything and come. I'm going now, but I will be back."

This time, I heard the kitchen door close, Ann's car start up and the sound of receding tires on gravel. Transfixed as a wax doll I remained seated until two tears slowly dribbled over my cheeks, dripped off my chin and landed on the back of my hand.

Stop that. Stop your sniveling. Sod 'em all. They can all go to hell.

Yeah, yeah, wallow some more, why don't you.

Shut up.

Go to your doctor then.

I'm not ill.

No, but you're sick of yourself aren't you?

As a mental cripple I struggled through the next week, doing only the bare necessities at work; fooling fellow workers that I was fine and deluding myself to thinking the same. I did speak briefly to my daughters and fobbed them off with vague platitudes. It was easy to brush away silent tears without a soul being any the wiser when I was not directly facing them, and if I managed not to sniff, so much the better. Dealing with Giles was even easier. He called in the middle of the week but "It had been a rough day, I had a headache and was going to bed early" no questions asked. Ann did not call.

However, by the end of the week I was physically and emotionally shattered, and thank God there were a few reasonable grey cells left to make me realize that I did indeed need help. I made an appointment to see my doctor. When the time came and I was sitting opposite this wonderful man who knew my entire family and had treated Megan for various ailments (mostly bruises and sprains) I collapsed like an imploded building.

"I've been expecting you," he said. "Today's the day you're going to feel better."

"No drugs." I garbled.

Stubborn as a bloody mule.

"Yes, drugs," he replied. "But these are no ordinary drugs, and I absolutely promise you that they will help as quickly as you can get this prescription filled. Even twenty-four hours from now you'll see a difference. How can you expect to get through this enormous tragedy by fighting it? I know you nurses don't believe in self-help," he looked at me with a wry smile. "You administer to the sick and never get ill yourself. I also know about the stigma of mental illness, but you're not paranoid, psychotic or a schizo."

"Just insane."

"Temporarily, yes."

For the first time since I could remember, I smiled. He pulled his chair closer, leaned forward and took both my hands in his.

"Look," he said. "Just try these pills for a month. They're very mild, not addictive and you can stop at any time, but they do have an accumulative effect, so let's say two weeks from now you should be feeling more like your old self."

I gave in.

"OK. Will they bring my sense of humor back?"

"Guaranteed."

We stood up and he gave me a bear like hug.

"I'm so sorry. This has to be the worst pain any mother could endure. Where's your husband by the way? Why isn't he with you?"

"He's around, but we're not doing very well and I can't cope with all that now. Who knows what's going to happen, so I'm lying low and letting the chips fall where they may."

"Good for you, that's probably the best thing. When in doubt do nothing, but if you should ever need counseling, don't forget I'm here for you both." He opened the door for me to leave. "Make another appointment for a couple of weeks' time and we'll talk some more. Take care."

"Thank you, I will."

Sure enough, in spite of my predilection to self-pity of late, either through the validity of the placebo effect or the fact the drugs were really working that fast, by the end of the week I was feeling better, so much so that guilt set in concerning my last conversation with Ann. How could I have been so rude to the one person who'd stood by me every minute of every day since Megan's death? Now I was extremely embarrassed and ashamed to face her. So, I wrote her a letter—I'm very sorry—ashamed of myself—went to the doctor—now on Prozac—please forgive me... all sad but true.

I heard nothing from Ann until the following Saturday, when there was such a commotion and honking of car horn in the driveway. Opening the kitchen door I saw her striding towards me, arms high in the air and frantically waving a sheet of paper.

"Don't say a word," she commanded. "I don't want to hear it." And she flung herself at me and gripped me in a vice-like hold until I thought a rib would break.

"I got your letter."

She was crying, I was crying.

"Welcome back, I've been so worried about you," she said when she eventually released me but still held me at arms length. "You must have been through hell—I know you have—do you feel better?"

"Much," I said. "But come on in. Do you think it's too early for a beer?"

She grinned. "Not for me it isn't."

So my dear friend and I sat in our usual chairs on the stoop and drank a six-pack between us—a liquid lunch if you like.

Thank you, God. How could I be so fortunate?

Chapter Twenty-Two

I called him Arthur. His father had been "Thatcher of Sarum" (Sarum being the old name for Salisbury, site of Stonehenge) so I named him "King Arthur of Wessex". (Wessex being the old name for the county of Wiltshire).

Cute, cute, fat and cute as all puppies should be. The one who waddled up to the edge of the pen and barked when I approached. The one who pushed his brothers and sisters out of the way for sole attention, and growled when challenged.

I already love you to bits, Arthur.

And so did Liza who must have looked a giant to him as she sniffed him over and then let him cuddle beside her.

The end of September brought Gail's birthday and I decided I wanted to surprise her this year. I sent her a card, but on the actual day purposely didn't call with birthday wishes. In cahoots with her boyfriend, Keith, and her roommate Keri, Giles and I drove up to Jacksonville at five in the afternoon armed with a bottle of champagne, flowers, a cake and dinner reservations at her favorite Japanese restaurant. Our daughter opened her door to us and shrieked. In the midst of hugs and hellos, she admitted her anger at the thought of being forgotten. It had taken the boyfriend and the roommate both to placate Gail and keep her home for the surprise. All was quickly forgiven, and the five of us had a thoroughly marvelous evening.

On the way back to Orlando both Giles and I were very quiet. *Did we really have nothing to say to each other any more?*

I stared out of the window to watch the trees disappear into the night and wondered how much longer we could continue like this. When alone we didn't talk about anything anymore; all communication had dwindled to a halt except for occasions such as this. It depressed me that my life had degenerated to naught, that I was a nonentity in Giles' life and the gap was widening with each passing day. I felt I had to say something to break this awful silence.

"Do you have plans for Thanksgiving?" I asked him.

"No," he replied. "I haven't thought that far ahead. What about you?"

"I think I'm going to have to take call for part of the holiday if I want Christmas off, and I definitely want that with Charles and Maggie coming out. I know Helen will be with Eric and his family in Ohio, and Gail will be flexible I'm sure, although if she knows I might have to work, she'll probably go home with Keith to Merritt Island. I don't really care about Thanksgiving anyway,"

It seemed we were destined to celebrate the national holiday apart whether I had to work or not. Giles didn't push for us to be together, and once more I felt I'd let him off the hook to do his own thing.

Giles' brother, Charles, and his wife, Maggie, were coming out to the States in December, to help us through the first Christmas without Megan. That holiday was still three months away but still I was dreading it. It was Megan's favorite and throughout her short life she'd always been like a five year old when it came to opening presents; the joy it had given me to watch her was incomparable.

I resorted to a trick of late—when I had sad thoughts like those, I tried to quickly and determinedly dismiss them from my brain. It worked only if I had something to distract me, and I knew I would have an eternal wait for consolation from Giles, which made me sadder. Was I meant to spend forever on this never-ending circle of false hope?

Turning into the driveway I redundantly said, "OK we're home. Thanks for driving me. It was a good evening."

"You're right it was. Good night then."

I felt like his grandmother having been taken from the nursing home for a special night out. I hoped at least Giles would have opened the car door for her. We were still a married couple, not dating, but there was no mention of future rendezvous not even a "see you around". Nothing, zilch, nada. These frigid conclusions to our rare evenings together and the fact we went our separate ways, upset me more than anything else.

Drop it. Don't let him get to you.

But it did get to me. When was the last time I laughed? When was the last time I had an optimistic thought? What hope did I have for the future? Was I married or single? It was a continuous uphill battle to stay sane. All the words from well-wishers came flooding back to me. "God has a plan" "God in his infinite wisdom" "God knows best" worthless platitudes for the loss of Megan, now applied to me.

Well hurry up God; get me out of this misery.

I took my turn on call for the hospital on Thanksgiving Day at Ann's house where I became swept up in the warmth of her wonderful family. Her Mom, sister and family, Kenny's brother and his wife and kids embraced me with love so genuine that for the first time in months I relaxed and allowed myself the luxury of self-indulgent bliss. It was a great day.

Back at home there was a message from Helen—would I please call her as soon as possible. With a shaking hand and racing heart I dialed the number—Eric's Mom's house in Ohio. Eric answered.

"Hey, Mom." He'd never called me "Mom" before. I heard him shout to Helen to come to the phone.

"Guess what, Mom?" Helen's breathless voice rang out. "It's official, Eric's asked me to marry him."

I slowly exhaled.

"Mom, are you there? Say something. Are you pleased?"

"I'm so absolutely delighted and presume you said yes. Congratulations, darling. I'm so happy for you. Have you set a date?"

"Probably not for at least another year. I've got to find a job, Eric must finish school and then we need to decide where we're going to live. But we're happy and we've had a great day today with all, and I mean all of Eric's family here for lunch. There were twenty-five of us sitting down at one time, not counting the kids; it was crazy. What about you? Did you have a good time at Ann's?"

"Yes, marvelous, thanks. And do you know I feel it was a kind of milestone for me. I enjoyed myself without guilt and haven't cried all day until now."

We laughed.

"Sorry, Mom."

"Don't be. These are tears of joy and relief. Relief the phone message wasn't a bad one and joy for your good news."

"Did you miss Dad?"

"No, not really. I've been on call all day, although I didn't have to go in, and he wanted to do his own thing and cook for his cronies, his homeless singles, he calls them. I wasn't prepared to join company with the likes of them, not after the way they treated me at Megan's memorial run. They sicken me."

"Well then it was probably just as well you spent the day apart. But we'll all be together for Christmas. Did you hear from Gail? I'd better go—we're playing charades. I love you, Mom. 'Bye."

"Cheerio, my darling. Thanks for calling and again congratulations, and tell Eric I said so. 'Bye."

For the first time since I could remember, I slept a peaceful dreamless sleep.

Chapter Twenty-Three

Christmas. Dear oh dear. Why were two big holidays so close to each other? I was on a roller coaster of emotions. Excited for Helen, Eric and Gail and very much looking forward to seeing Charles and Maggie. On the other hand, my heart was only mildly interested in buying presents and I rote shopped for groceries. Everyone would be coming to my house for dinner but somehow I didn't mind the prospect of cooking. I'd done it every year since dot, and had become very protective of my role—almost challenging anyone else to do better. A glass or three of sherry, convivial chatter from the kids and guests, and a general air of excitement eased the chore of peeling spuds on Christmas morning.

My brothers called from England wishing us well, although my older brother, Michael told us he wasn't feeling so good—a touch of flu. Shame. By midday, miraculously the meal came together as it should, so that at one o'clock, seven of us were eating the traditional fare washed down with plenty of wine or spirits or both.

The crutch of booze—I felt no pain. I watched Giles carve the turkey—I saw glasses raised in a toast—I heard Charles say the blessing—felt the nudge of an elbow when Maggie lifted her plate to be served, and I thought of Megan, my darling, darling child whose voice would have been the loudest at this table. I looked at my two daughters across from me, both caught my eye and both knew.

I'm here, Mom. Don't cry for me. Enjoy your day.

In the evening after opening our presents we were joined by Matt Cooper. He'd long had a passion for Helen, not reciprocated by her, although she enjoyed his company as a friend. I thought she had a particularly wicked glint in her eye when she casually asked Matt if he remembered Eric, her fiancé. God bless him, he didn't flinch but hugged her and shook Eric's hand in best wishes.

Matt was an added bonus to our group as he joined with Gail when we played Pictionary. I sat at Giles's feet and as a pair we were in complete unison, won many rounds and forged ahead of our enemies. I basked in the familiarity and so enjoyed laughing in friendly competition. Charles was the perfectionist and continued drawing long after the round was finished to whoops and hollers from Helen and Eric who couldn't have cared less that they were hardly off square one of the board. However it was Gail, the absolute master of quick drawing and even better at guessing answers from squiggly lines who eventually won the game for her and Matt.

Again I thought of Megan and how she had loved and hated this game.

"Can't you see—that's a bull with a ring through its nose. Anyone could tell that's the Earth and not a balloon—and that's supposed to be. . ." as her poor partner whoever it was, tried desperately to decipher her hieroglyphics.

Megs, we had a good game, but I woefully miss your shameful antics.

Helen brewed coffee and Gail poured liqueurs, but I'd had enough, so quietly took myself off to my darkened bedroom and lay on my bed. I needed Roger. I needed the warmth of his fur against my face and the reassuring sound of purring in my ear. I needed to tell him we'd had a good day and how I still missed Megan so very much. He'd understand, but he must have been outside.

A little while later there was a soft knock on the open door. I looked up to see Giles silhouetted in the gap.

"Are you all right?" he asked.

"Yes, I'm OK. It's been a long day and I'm tired now."

"Well, I think we'll be going soon. It's been great, terrific food as usual. Thanks for everything."

I stood up.

"You're welcome and I hope to see you all during the week. Don't forget we're going to Mario's restaurant with Ann and Kenny for New Year's."

"No, I haven't forgotten."

The physical awkwardness between us had returned. Embrace? Kiss? Get naked?

I was long past caring and accepted the peck on my cheek for the silly gesture it was. Matt left at the same time as Giles, Maggie and Charles.

"Great day, Mom. Thanks."

"Yes, thanks Mom, you did a super job." Gail stood with her arm around my shoulder. "Megan would have been so proud. At one time I really thought she was here."

"She was," I said. "Do you honestly think she would miss this? I'm going to bed now and finish clearing up in the morning. Good night. It has been a wonderful day but I'm glad it's all over. See you in the morning."

"We'll tidy up, Mom. Goodnight."

Four days later on Monday the twenty-ninth December, I received a phone call from England. It was Angela my sister-in-law.

"I thought I'd better ring you to tell you Michael's in hospital."

"Oh no. What's wrong?"

"Nobody seems to know exactly. He hasn't been feeling well

for about a week—low-grade temperature—night sweats, nothing specific. Mike thinks it's just a cold or even flu but Dr. Willis wanted him admitted to keep an eye on him and do more tests."

"I know he wasn't feeling well when you called us on Christmas Day. Poor thing. Thanks for calling me. Give him my love and I hope he gets better soon. You will let me know won't you?"

"Yes, for sure I will. Bye now."

"'Bye."

I hung up the phone. Angela and I weren't bosom pals but I gave her enormous credit for being a good wife and mother to their three children. Michael and I had remained close even though I hadn't seen much of them over the past few years. He was terribly upset at Megan's death, calling me every day for a week, wishing he could do more to help.

OK well, I had great faith in the British Health Service. He was in good hands.

Late the next day, Angela called me again to tell me Michael had been taken to the operating theatre.

"He's bleeding."

"From where?"

"Nobody seems to know for sure, but the surgeon seemed to think Mike had a bleeding stomach ulcer," Angela said. "Or maybe they aren't telling me the whole story."

"Would you like me to talk to them? Obviously I have a better understanding of the surgical lingo and could give you a clearer picture."

"Thanks," she said. "But let's wait and see. He's back on the ward now and I'm going to bed- it's one o'clock in the morning here. There's not much anyone can do at this time of night, so I'll ring you tomorrow with an update when I've spoken to the doctors again."

"OK." I said. "I appreciate you calling me, and if there's anything

I can do to help, don't hesitate to ask. Poor old boy. Is he in a lot of pain?"

"No, he's knocked out pretty well. I must go—I'll be in touch. 'Bye."

"Goodnight. Take care."

Hmm. What could be wrong with my brother? Having assisted with operations on hundreds of belly cases in my career my mind went into overtime thinking of all the possibilities of blood loss. Were flu like symptoms an indication for ulcers? I couldn't remember. He must have had other signs to warrant surgery, and how could the surgeons stop the hemorrhage if they didn't know from whence it came? I was beginning to worry a little.

All these thoughts were put on hold as I prepared to go out and celebrate the New Year. For nine months since Megan's death I lived only one day at a time, but yesterday's gone and now I was looking forward to the future—it had to be better next year. Kenny (Ann's husband) had a brother who managed a fabulous Italian restaurant and it had been arranged that we all go for dinner there and later when the restaurant was closed to the public, we would stay and have a private family celebration to see the New Year in. It was a perfect set up as I didn't want another party at my house and surely didn't want to go to Giles' apartment even though Charles and Maggie were staying with him. I didn't fancy leaving his place at one o'clock in the morning to go home alone. It was all so embarrassing. Besides I was on my own again as Helen and Eric had returned up north and Gail was with Keith.

When I arrived, Ann and Kenny greeted me and to my surprise Giles, Charles and Maggie were already there too. Was it my turn to be late? No matter, after a couple of glasses of wine and the most splendid meal of the best Italian food, we were all relaxed and content. My thoughts drifted first to my brother, Michael, in England. *Hang in there, Mike*. And then to Megan *let go, let live* and on to the various New Year's Eves Giles and I had spent together — some of the best ones were in Zambia and Zimbabwe, twenty years ago or more, where we were often forced to stay the night because of the dangerous political situation then, causing unsafe roads and curfews.

I glanced at Giles engaged in animated conversation with his brother. Still a handsome man in spite of graying hair and deep wrinkle lines around his mouth. I was always attracted to his hands — long slender fingers — artists' hands, and I looked at them now, one wrapped around a beer glass, the other gesturing in the air to press home a point. Do I still love you? How had we drifted so far apart? What had gone so wrong that we were almost strangers? We were a married couple tied by grief, not love.

Later when the restaurant had emptied leaving immediate family and friends to party, I stood alone. It was almost midnight and I watched the television over the bar showing the usual year's end revelry from Times Square in New York.

I heard Ann's voice behind me, "go to her," and shortly thereafter felt Kenny's arms around me and I gratefully leaned back against him for the comfort I desperately needed.

"Thank you." I whispered and dared not face him as tears seeped over my lids and slowly ran down my face.

I love you Kenny. I love you Ann. I love you Helen, I love you Gail. I love you Megan. I love the world. . .

Driving home on my own, gave me time to reflect on the evening. Another emotional hurdle had come and gone — another holiday without Megan and here I was surviving, existing, breathing and numb.

The light was flashing on the answering machine but before I could retrieve the message the telephone rang startling me at such a late hour. It was Angela.

"Sorry to be ringing you so late."

"No, no," I assured her. "I've just come in—what's up? How's Mike?"

"They've taken him back to the operating theatre—he's bleeding again—he's there now—it's really bad," a long pause, "they don't think he's going to make it," she finished in a voice barely above a whisper

"What! What do you mean he's not going to make it? You mean he's going to die? No! No! No! Do they know where the hemorrhage is? Surely the doctors can do something." I could hear my own voice raised in panic. *This can't be happening.*

"Where are you, Angela?"

"I'm at the hospital. Caroline's (their daughter) with me."

"Oh God—oh dear—I feel so helpless—I don't know what to do—or say."

"There's nothing you can do," said Angela. "Just pray."

"I will. Look my dear; know that my thoughts and prayers are with you—constantly. I wish I was there but glad you're not on your own. Caroline is always such a comfort to you and I know how much she loves her Dad. Don't lose heart—call me."

"I will. 'Bye." She was gone.

God, what the hell is going on? God, now You listen to me—what do You think you're doing? You can't let Michael die—it's not possible. Why in Your name—hasn't this family suffered enough? And just when my faith in You is restored—no, please—I beg You...I don't think I can take anymore...

I dozed in and out of sleep for the rest of the night and finally abandoned the idea completely by six. New Year's Day Nineteen

Ninety-eight and I was sick of this year already. Michael, my dear sweet brother lay dying? It couldn't be—it musn't be. God, You can't be so cruel, it's not fair.

Life's not fair, nah nah nah nah nah nah.

Yes, but why me?

Why not me?

Giles had gone to his office even though it was a holiday, and his brother and sister-in-law arrived mid-morning at my house.

"Any news from England?" asked Maggie.

"Yes." I told her of the previous conversation with Angela. Being a nurse too, Maggie was just as stunned as I was, and together we tried to reason out the few facts we had for Michael's case.

"None of it makes sense." I finally declared and stepped outside for a breath of fresh air. It was good to be with Liza and Arthur, now a four month old puppy and an instant reminder that there was a shred of joy in my life.

Charles and Maggie took me out to lunch in Mount Dora, a quaint little town north of Orlando known for its antiques, and for a short time my mind was distracted. But on returning home the dreaded blinking light was on my answering machine.

David, my younger brother. "Call me as soon as you get this."

I called—I knew what was coming but I let him tell me anyway.

"Bad news I'm afraid," he began. "Michael died at one o'clock today."

Chapter Twenty-Four

"Go, we'll take care of the animals. You need to be there. Go."

Hasty arrangements—British Airways—my brother David at Heathrow, and there I was in England on a bitterly cold January day attending Michael's funeral, on his birthday no less. He was fifty-six years old, in his prime and no one could give me the cause of his death. But for the life of me, I could not cry. So sapped by tragedy—all defenses down and burdened by enormous grief during the last nine months, I had nothing left to give. I drowned out all sound, stared straight ahead and pondered this phenomenon.

I must cry—what will people think? C,mon summon a tear.

It would be eight days later that we received notice of why Michael died. The post-mortem was clear, even if our understanding of how this could happen wasn't. He had contracted a very rare virus that had attacked his heart, eventually causing it to virtually burst. *Meningeal-coccal cardiomyopathy* was the medical term and once I heard that, I knew the poor soul hadn't stood a chance.

I stayed with David and his wife, Carol and during this time Giles called me twice from Florida. The second time I really did not want to talk to him, but as my brother had no idea of my marital troubles (no one had ever been divorced on either side); I put on a good show of normality even though my half of the conversation was short and tense.

In spite of the circumstances for my visit, and the miserable weather, I was reluctant to return to Florida. I was safe in my family's arms in England and didn't have to face my future alone.

Somewhere mid-Atlantic at thirty-five thousand feet, in the sunlight above clouds, I knew. My marriage to Giles would have to end.

Megan. Thatcher. My brother. My marriage.

I found my tears.
I found my life.

Closure

If I close my eyes do I lose sight of her? No, quite the opposite-
—she becomes vivid in my imagination, her very existence a breath
away.

Why the need for closure? What is this word?

Cessation. Discontinuance. To shut out or bring to an end. A
dead stop; yes it was definitely that.

What am I to put to rest?

Her molecular being has long gone, her soul I'm sure is on the
second circuit of the everlasting track.

What am I to close? That she once was? Am I ending my grief?

Sorrow has a beginning, but its end is limitless. How can you
cap off the emotional well of a lifetime of memories? The broken
heart still bleeds. The agony of departure is still real.

Suffering diminishes slowly, and at times imperceptibly.
Sometimes it is so encompassing and lasting, it feels like terror. It
can never be erased as abruptly as the word closure might suggest.

It's over. We've neatly packed up all prostrations of grief into a
coffin labeled "closed".

Cease, desist—no more. Enough!

Closure, a nonsensical word of modern times for the convenience
of others.

A pox on those others.

Conclusion? I now know what it is.

It's in the instant of knowing there is no death.

I don't walk on eggshells anymore.

Post Script

Five years after Megan's death, long after my divorce, I went to visit Gail who was now living in California.

On the flight back, approaching Florida, the turbulence became very strong, something quite normal in summertime with daily storms.

I was sitting in a middle seat gripping the arm of the divider with one hand and caressing the little crystal angel pin on my lapel, with the other. Helen had given me the pin at Megan's memorial service many years ago, and I always wore it when flying.

I glanced to my right, across the aisle and the other three seats to the opposite window. Outside, it was almost black with thunderclouds. I could hardly believe my eyes to see Megan, head back, mouth open, long brown hair streaming out behind her, seemingly hanging on to what I thought were handle bars of some sort.

She was laughing and alternately looking ahead and then across to me. Every time the plane dipped into a pocket of air she would ride it out and I could hear her say, "this is awesome, Mom." She laughed some more and bent lower over her handles to face the next wave of forceful air.

I grinned at her and almost raised my hand in a salutation, until I realized how futile that would be.

Boom! Another bump and a drop as the plane was repeatedly buffeted by the weather. Megan continued to ride out the storm, "Mom, this is so great, but don't worry, you'll be fine," and she was gone.

Megan loves to fly.

In Loving Memory of
Megan Leigh Paget-Wilkes

1978~1997